recent discovery of more manuscripts and the publication of better editions of his writings have stimulated an extensive reinterpretation of Hobbes's ideas and goals.

The essays cover four aspects of Hobbes's thought: his political theory, his views on religion, his moral philosophy, and his theory of motion and philosophical method. With the exception of John Dewey's "The Motivation of Hobbes's Political Philosophy," all the essays were written especially for this book. The other essays and authors are "The Anglican Theory of Salvation in Hobbes" by Paul Johnson, San Bernardino State College; "Some Puzzles in Hobbes" by Ralph Ross, Scripps College, The Claremont Colleges; "The Piety of Hobbes" by Herbert W. Schneider, emeritus professor of Columbia University and Claremont Graduate School, The Claremont Colleges; "The Generation of the Public Person" by Theodore Waldman, Harvey Mudd College, The Claremont Colleges; and "The *Philosophia Prima* of Thomas Hobbes" by Craig Walton, University of Nevada.

Thomas Hobbes in His Time

The University of Minnesota Press
gratefully acknowledges the support for its program
of the Andrew W. Mellon Foundation.
This book is one of those in whose financing
the Foundation's grant played a part.

THOMAS HOBBES
IN HIS TIME

Edited by

Ralph Ross

Herbert W. Schneider

Theodore Waldman

UNIVERSITY OF MINNESOTA PRESS

MINNEAPOLIS

CONTENTS

THOMAS HOBBES: CHRONOLOGY OF CHIEF EVENTS AND WRITINGS

1588	Born at Malmesbury. His birth was premature; according to him his mother was terrorized by the approach of the Spanish Armada. "Fear was my twin."
1608	Baccalaureate in classical studies at Oxford University; his college, Magdalen, was under Puritan administration.
1608–28; 1631–40; 1652–79	He was a member of the household of the Earl of Devonshire, William Cavendish; first as tutor, then secretary, traveling companion. The major part of Hobbes's papers are housed at the Chatsworth estate of the Cavendish family. They also had a London residence.
1610–13	First trip to France and Italy.
1623–24 (approx.)	Secretary to Francis Bacon at his estate in St. Albans. Hobbes translated some of the *Essays* into Latin. Walks and conversations with Bacon in the garden; social events attended by literary notables.
1628	Published translation of the *Eight Books of the Peloponnesian War* by Thucydides. "Interpreted with faith and diligence immediately out of the Greek."
1628–31	Second voyage to the Continent.
1634–37	Third voyage to the Continent. Met Galileo in Florence, began correspondence with scientists, and in-

tensive work on geometry and optics. "A Short Tract on First Principles" reflects his attempts to adapt his Oxford studies to the methods of the Padua School and Galileo, to William Harvey's ideas on motions in vital bodies, and to the theories of Light of the Oxford Franciscans, Grosseteste and Roger Bacon. This Tract was first published in 1889 as an appendix to Tönnies's edition of *The Elements of Law.*

1636   In a letter to the Earl of Newcastle he discusses the foundations for a genuine science of law. Following the Earl's suggestion he begins to work on this foundation.

Mar. 9, 1640   He writes in his Epistle Dedicatory to the Earl of Newcastle of his work "The Elements of Law Natural and Politic" as follows:

From the two principal parts of our nature, Reason and Passion, have proceeded two kinds of learning: mathematical and dogmatical. . . . They that have written of justice and policy in general, do all invade each other and themselves with contradiction. To reduce this doctrine to the rules and infallibility of reason, there is no way, but first to put such principles down for a foundation, as passion not mistrusting, may not seek to displace; and afterward to build thereon the truth of cases in the law of nature (which hitherto have been built in the air) by degrees, till the whole be inexpugnable. . . . By your command I have here put into method those principles. . . . I present this to your Lordship for the true and only foundation for such a science.

The two parts of this treatise are Part I, Concerning Men as Persons Natural; Part II, Concerning Men as a Body Politic. There is no reference here to a larger work, *Elements of Philosophy* in three volumes, into which he embodied these Elements of Law, as *De Homine* and *De Cive*; the other volume to be *De Corpore.*

Nov. 1640   Fled from England to Paris. He lived in a convent presided over by Mersenne, a critic of Descartes, who published almost immediately the *Objectiones.*

1641   *Objectiones in Cartesii de Prima Philosophia, Meditationes* (Paris and Amsterdam).

1642   *Elementorum Philosophiae, Sectio Tertia, De Cive* (Paris, printed privately). The Epistle Dedicatory to this work is dated November 1641. There is other evidence that he had been planning the three-volume work during the late 1630's.

1643   *De Motu, Loco, et Tempore* (published later).

1644   *Tractatus Opticus* (Paris, published by Mersenne). During these years he was cooperating with the Ramus Professor of Mathematics at the Royal College, Gilles Personne de Roberval, who was also working in Optics and on Grosseteste's theory of Light.

1645   Charles, Prince of Wales, arrived in exile in Paris. Hobbes was assigned to give him lessons in mathematics.

1647   *Elementa Philosophica de Cive* (Amsterdam).

1649 and   *Human Nature* (London). *De Corpore Politico, or the*
1650   *Elements of Law, Moral and Politic* (London). These were the poorly edited and separated two parts of the *Elements of Law*, which Hobbes had written in 1640 and left with friends when he fled.

1651   *Philosophical Rudiments concerning Government and Society* (London). Hobbes's own translation of *De Cive*. The subtitle is *A Dissertation concerning Man in His Several Habitudes and Respects, as the Member of a Society, First Secular and Then Sacred*.
Leviathan, or the Matter, Form, and Power of a Commonwealth, Ecclesiastical and Civil (London). This edition contains the famous frontispiece representing the public person with the symbols of civil and ecclesiastical authority.

1652   Returns to his home at Chatsworth with the Earl of Devonshire.

1654   *Of Liberty and Necessity* (London). Written in 1646 in private discussion with Bishop Bramhall, and published without the consent of Hobbes.

1655   *Elementa Philosophiae Sectio Prima de Corpore*.

1656   *The Questions concerning Liberty, Necessity and Chance,
        Clearly Stated and Debated between Dr. Bramhall, Bishop
        of Derry, and Thomas Hobbes, of Malmesbury* (London).
        Elements of Philosophy, The First Section concerning Body
        (London).
        *Six Lessons to the Professors of the Mathematics . . . in
        the University of Oxford* (London).

1658   *De Homine, sive Elementorum Philosophiae Sectio Secunda*
        (London). He delayed the publication of this last of
        his three-volume work, in order to include revisions
        in Optics and the theory of Sense Perception.

1666   He composed *Behemoth*, which was published post-
(approx.) humously because the king forbade its publication
        on the ground of its "inflammatory" tendency.

1668   *Leviathan* (Amsterdam). This Latin translation by
        Hobbes contains a few changes, e.g., elimination of
        a passage in Book IV which favored independent
        churches.

1672   *Lux Mathematica* (London).

1673   Composed the Dialogue on the Common Law, pub-
(approx.) lished in 1681.

1675   Translations of *The Iliad* and *Odyssey* by Homer.

1678   *Decameron Physiologicum, or Ten Dialogues of Natural
        Philosophy.*

Dec. 1679 Death of Thomas Hobbes.

1680   *Behemoth, or The Long Parliament. Dialogue of the Civil
        Wars of England* (William Crooke, London).

1681   *A Dialogue between a Philosopher and a Student of the
        Common Laws of England* (London).
        The Whole Art of Rhetoric (London).

1682   *Seven Philosophical Problems and Two Propositions of
        Geometry* (London).

Sir William Molesworth published the complete works in sixteen
volumes: *The English Works of Thomas Hobbes*, 11 vols., 1839–45; *The
Latin Works*, 5 vols., 1845ff. There have been amended editions
since then of some, and several works published recently for the
first time.

Thomas Hobbes in His Time

INTRODUCTION
by Ralph Ross, Herbert W. Schneider,
Theodore Waldman

THOMAS HOBBES has again become the center of lively discussion among philosophers, historians, and political theorists. Both as a participant in a revolutionary commonwealth and as a student of the science of human nature, Hobbes has achieved a new relevance to the contemporary world. Moralists are now apt to place him in the twentieth century, and historians are apt to portray him as an antique. The aim of these essays is to get an accurate account of how radical Hobbes was in his own revolutionary century.

The essays are the fruit of years of cooperative study, going back to the days when John Dewey called our attention to Hobbes's interest in transforming the courts of common law into courts of equity, a policy which he carried over from his association with the lord chancellor Francis Bacon. The recent discovery of more manuscripts and the publication of better editions of his writings have stimulated an extensive reinterpretation of Hobbes's ideas and aims. These essays deal with some of the controversial topics of current discussion about Hobbes, but they keep him in the context of his own time. Even then Hobbes was subject to attacks from many sides. Although the stereotype of "Hobbism" which grew up during four centuries of revolution-

3

ary developments is now generally rejected by scholars, new stereotypes are emerging. To counteract these, our essays attempt to understand Hobbes in terms of his own day.

The first and fourth essays describe the political issues which Hobbes faced: his criticism of the common law courts in favor of courts of equity, and his theory of the constitution and institution of a legitimate commonwealth. The second and third essays examine his ideas on scientific principles and methods. The fifth and sixth essays deal with his "latitudinarian" defense of the Church of England and with the religious aspects of the civil war in Britain. In the history of each of these three fields (political reconstruction, scientific progress, and wars of religion) during the seventeenth century Hobbes stands out as a philosopher who sought rational ways of dealing with highly controversial practical problems, and as a man whose disdain for compromise caused him to be attacked from all sides. Like Socrates, he was a "gadfly," or, to use the symbol with which King Charles II referred to him, he was a "bear." He pleased no party and no sect in his own time, but his literary art and critical wit make his writings good reading and his philosophy is relevant in our century of discovery and strife.

During Hobbes's life the theories of divine right, of feudal birthrights, and of hereditary sovereignty were becoming antiquated. With the rapid rise of commercial capital and power, the ideas of the landed aristocracy appeared artificial to the bourgeoisie. Status was giving way to contract; one's fixed position in society was being replaced by agreement and exchange of goods and services. The quarrels of rival lords were being subordinated to international rivalry and wars. Within the churches there was an increasing emphasis among congregations and parishes on "covenants," both "under God" and in the communion of saints.

In this situation new conceptions of commonwealth and legitimacy were evidently needed, both in theory and in fact. Hobbes's critique of common law in favor of contract law and his advocacy of sovereignty by "institution" or constitution were radical, because his innovations were neither partisan nor compromises. He attacked the basic concepts rationally without regard to tradition: He rejected the idea that man is a compound of matter and spirit; he reconstructed the meaning of *ius naturale* in terms of empirical principles of peace.

By long tradition man's nature had been considered to be dual: half matter, half spirit. Both halves were conceived as substances, one material, one spiritual. Hobbes denied all this and enthusiastically accepted the new science of "bodies in motion." Bodies are individual beings naturally in motion among other bodies, each with specific energies, "endeavors," and capacities. In the case of living bodies, which were Hobbes's chief concern, they are endowed with both external movements and "internal motions" (motives, emotions). Similarly, if living bodies are in any sense also "spiritual bodies," spirit, like life, must be embodied. It is not itself a body or substance, but an attribute or "accident" of certain bodies. Hence the basic moral problem is how to lead a spiritual life on earth among other bodies. The church had regarded the "spiritual body of Christ" or "the communion of saints" as the solution to this problem. Hobbes rejected this flatly: "There are no spiritual bodies on earth." But there can be "bodies politick." And on this basis, which the bishops called "atheism," Hobbes constructed a rival theory of human nature and commonwealth. He wrote it first under the head of *Elements of Law*, and then he projected a more ambitious system in three volumes: *De Homine, De Corpore, De Cive*. But before he could compose these three treatises, in the heat of civil war he gave classic expression to the same philosophy in his *Leviathan*, written in exile but heralding his return to the commonwealth in England.

The message in *Leviathan* was eloquent and intensely relevant to his fellow citizens. Every man is a body, but to become complete and secure he must enter into a "body politick." He becomes a citizen by covenant. As a body, he remains subject to the natural government of God Almighty. He can exist as a citizen in a commonwealth, which rests on a covenant. The church is not such a body. However, a Christian may have faith that eventually a "heavenly kingdom" will be established by Christ on earth, in which the principles of justice and peace will be law. Meanwhile, such "heavenly law" or *ius naturale* must be discovered and formulated rationally on the basis of human experience. The principles of this law Hobbes claimed to have discovered, and this he regarded as his greatest achievement.

In addition, he offered his time many ideas so challenging to accepted belief that he was easily misrepresented and was attacked in many quarters as "the monster of Malmesbury." He regarded consent as necessary to obligation, and so to civil society, "there being no Obligation on any man, which ariseth not from some act of his own; for all men equally, are by Nature Free." He saw that consent needed to be underscored by a theory of authority, since the right to command did not follow simply from consent. That the body politic be able to act required a voice and to be a voice was to be an "author," from whom came authority. There were secondary voices, to be sure, voices of "actors," but they spoke the words of an author, not their own. The "voice of the people" was some one or some body, a man or an assembly, authorized to speak in their name as their representative. Consent, then, formed the body politic and authorization gave it a voice.

Although Hobbes converted the notion that the king can do no wrong into one in which he could do no injustice, he distinguished the authority with which one acts (its legal justice or injustice) from the wisdom with which one acts (its felicity or foolishness). And he is clear that although the sovereign, being the source of law, cannot by definition act unjustly, he can act immorally: he "may in diverse ways transgress against the other laws of nature, as by cruelty, iniquity, contumely, and other like vices." Lawful government might on occasion be bad government and its consequences destructive to the commonwealth. Thus, though there was no right to rebellion, there well might be conditions for which the sovereign was responsible that in fact drove men to rebellion. To overlook this aspect of Hobbes's teaching is to know him inadequately.

One might mention that Hobbes also developed a view of punishment which was rehabilitative rather than retributive. It was for a future good rather than a past wrong that it was to be directed, and cruelty was not to be part of it. Hobbes had a fine sense for distinctions, but with it a genuine sense of charity. They appear together when he says such things as: "And to Robbe a poore man, is a greater crime than to robbe a rich man; because 'tis to the poore a more sensible dammage."

Lastly, Hobbes's view that sovereigns stand to each other as men in a state of nature suggests that the laws of nature which guided men in their search for a common authority could also be a basis for a law of nations or a common authority among nations. It is true that he did not explore this possibility, but it speaks to us from one deeply troubled age to another.

The following essays explain in detail how Hobbes dealt with some of his problems, what difficulties and puzzles he met, and how he changed his mind from time to time in order to improve his "method." All the essays in this book were written for it and have not been published before, except for the piece by John Dewey which appeared in a publication of the Columbia University Department of Philosophy, but has not been reprinted until now.

THE MOTIVATION OF HOBBES'S POLITICAL PHILOSOPHY

by John Dewey

IT IS THE OBJECT of this essay to place the political philosophy of Hobbes in its own historic context. The history of thought is peculiarly exposed to an illusion of perspective. Earlier doctrines are always getting shoved, as it were, nearer our own day. We are familiar with the intellectual struggles of our own time and are interested in them. It is accordingly natural to envisage earlier thought as part of the same movement or as its forerunner. We then forget that that earlier period had its own specific problems, and we proceed to assimilate its discussions to our present interest. Hobbes has been especially subject to this temporal displacement. For over a century the chief question in social philosophy has centered about the conflict between individual freedom and public and institutional control. The central position of the theory of sovereignty in Hobbes's thought has made it easy to translate his political philosophy into terms of this debate; the issue which was really acute in his day—the conflict of church and state—now lacks actuality for English and American writers at least.

I

To prove this statement as to the central issue of Hobbes's day would require more than the space allotted to this paper. In general, I can only refer to the voluminous political discussions of the seventeenth century and to the overt history of England during the time of the civil wars. Specifically, let me note the admirable studies of Mr. Figgis.[1] They are enough to relieve my statement from any charge of exaggeration. Some quotations from Mr. Figgis will, then, be used to introduce the discussion. He points out that the controversy regarding the divine right of kings belongs to a day when politics, by common consent, was a branch of theology, and goes on to say, "All men demanded some form of divine authority for any theory of government . . . Until the close of the seventeenth century, the atmosphere of the supporters of popular rights is as theological as that of the upholders of the Divine Right of Kings."[2] And again, "There is no more universal characteristic of the political thought of the seventeenth century than the notion of non-resistance to authority. 'To bring the people to obedience' is the object of writers of all schools. When resistance is preached, it is resistance to some authority regarded as subordinate. Nor is the resistance permitted at the pleasure or judgment of private individuals. It is allowed only as a form of obedience, as executing the commands of some superior and ultimate authority, God, or the Pope, and the Law."[3]

In other words, everybody worked upon an assumption of a supreme authority, of law as command by this authority, and duty as ultimately obedience. Not these conceptions, but rather the special content given them, mark off Hobbes. There was, of course, a party which opposed such centralization as Hobbes argued for, but the opposition was not in the name of the individual, but of something very different, the people.

So far as I can discover, the term *people* still had its meaning fixed by the traditional significance of *Populus*—a meaning very different from that of *plebs* or the French *peuple*. This notion, as defined, say, by Cicero, was a commonplace among the "civilians" and those trained in scholastic philosophy. In Cicero's words, the people is "not every gathering of men, assembled in any way whatsoever, but is the multitude associated by a common sense of justice and by a common interest." It is a *universitas*, not a *societas*, much less a mere aggregate of individuals. And the appeal of the upholders of popular against royal government was to the *authority* of this organized body, of which the Commons was frequently (but not always) taken to be the representative. The following words from Lawson, taken from *An Examination of the Political Part of Mr. Hobbes, His Leviathan* (1657) are worth quoting: "The liberty which the English have challenged and obtained with so much expense of blood is . . . that which is due unto us by the constitution of the State, Magna Charta, the Laws, and the Petition of Right. It is but the liberty of subjects, not sovereigns; when he hath said all he can, we are not willing to be slaves or subject ourselves to Kings as Absolute Lords. . . . By liberty Aristotle meant such a privilege as every subject might have in a free state . . . where it is to be noted that one and the same person who is a subject, and at the best but a Magistrate, hath a share in the sovereign power. Yet this he hath not as a single person, but as one person jointly with the whole body or major part at least of the people" (pp. 67–68). This correlativity of three things: the people, a society organized through laws and especially through the fundamental law, or constitution, and liberty is in marked opposition to Locke's conceptions of a natural right or authority found in the individual himself. It is not, I think, paradoxical to say that Locke derived this conception of a natural right belonging to the individual as such from Hobbes rather than from Hobbes's popular opponents.

It is noteworthy that Cumberland, the chief systematic opponent of Hobbes on rationalistic grounds, objects to the latter's political philosophy because "Hobbes's principles overthrow the Foundations of all Government"; they would not suffer any man to enter into civil society; they excite subjects to rebellion. In short, it is Hobbes's psychological and moral individualism rather than his theory of sovereignty to which objection is taken. The same is true of a much less effective writer, Tenison, in his *Creed of Mr. Hobbes Examined* (1670). He says that since Hobbes identifies the law of nature with the counsels of self-interest "the Fundamentals of your Policy are hay and stubble, and apter to set all things into blaze than to support government" (p. 156); and again, "Woe to all the Princes on earth, if this doctrine be true and becometh popular; if the multitude believe this, the Prince . . . can never be safe from the spears and barbed irons which their ambition and presumed interest will provide." Hobbes's principles, in their appeal to self-interest, are but "seeds of sedition" (pp. 170–171). That Hobbes himself was aware that, as matter of fact, a government is not likely to retain enough strength to secure obedience unless it has regard to the commonweal, will appear in the sequel—though naturally he never made this moral explicit.

Let us hear from Mr. Figgis again. "It is true that with the possible exception of Hobbes, all the political theorists up to the end of the seventeenth century either have religion as the basis of their system, or regard the defense or supremacy of some form of faith as their main object."[4] Now Hobbes is precisely the exception which proves the rule. He is theological in motive and context in the sense that he is deliberately anti-theological. Along with his exclusive self-interest doctrine, it was his theory of a secular basis for sovereignty, not the doctrine of a supreme authority, which brought him into disrepute.[5] His familiar title was atheist, so that even the royalists who might be supposed, on purely political grounds to welcome his support, found it necessary to disclaim him. Compare the following from a contemporary letter: "All honest men who are lovers of monarchy, are very glad that the King hath at last banisht his court that father of atheists Mr. Hobbes, who it is said hath rendered all the queen's court, and very many of the Duke of York's family, atheists."[6] In the apologetic dedication of his *Seven Philosophical Problems* to the king after the Restoration in 1662, Hobbes in defending himself against this charge says of his *Leviathan*, "There is nothing in it against episcopacy. I can not therefore imagine what reason any episcopal man can have to speak of me, as I hear some of them do, as of an atheist or man of no religion, *unless it be for making the authority of the church depend wholly upon the regal power.* "In the words which I have italicized Hobbes flaunts his ground of offense.

II

Postponing, for the moment, the important point in Hobbes, his attempt to secularize morals and politics, I take up his own sayings regarding the immediate occasion of his political writings. Croom Robertson and Tönnies have made it clear that the first of his writings[7] dates from 1640 and is substantially what we have in his *Human Nature* and *De Corpore Politico.* In his *Considerations upon the Reputation of T. Hobbes* (1662) Hobbes says this little treatise "did set forth and demonstrate that the said power and rights were inseparably annexed to the sovereignty," and that the treatise was so much talked of, although it was not printed, that if the king had not dissolved Parliament, it would have brought him into danger of his life.[8] There is here, indeed, no reference to just what the points were in the quarrel about the regal power, but his *Behemoth; or the Long Parliament* leaves no doubt. There he says that the Parliament of 1640 "desired the whole and absolute sovereignty. . . . For this was the design of the Presbyterian ministers, who taking themselves to be, by divine right, the only lawful governors of the Church, endeavored to bring the same form of government into the civil state. And as the spiritual laws were to be made by their synods, so the civil laws should be made by the House of Commons."[9] And at the beginning of this work, in stating the causes of the corruption of the people which made the civil wars possible, he puts first the Presbyterians, second the Papists, and third the Independents.[10]

In the *Considerations* already referred to he says he "wrote and published his book *De Cive,* to the end that all nations which should hear what you and your Con-Coventanters were doing in England, might detest you." Not less significant is his letter, from Paris, in 1641 to the Earl of Devonshire. He says, "I am of the opinion that ministers ought to minister rather than govern; at least, that all Church government depends on the state, and authority of the kingdom, without which there can be no unity in the church. Your lordship may think this but a Fancy of Philosophy, but I am sure that Experience teacheth thus much, that the dispute for (the word is variously read preference and precedence) between the spiritual and civil power, has of late more than any other thing in the world been the cause of civil war."[11] Of the *Leviathan*, he says: "The cause of my writing that book was the consideration of what the ministers before, and in the beginning of the civil war, by their preaching and writing did contribute thereunto" (VII, 35). And it may be worth noting that considerably over one-half of the *Leviathan* is explicitly devoted to the bearing of religious and scriptural matters upon politics as they touch upon the relation of church and the civil power.

In his controversy with "the egregious professors of the mathematics in the University of Oxford" he remarks of the *De Cive*: "You know that the doctrine therein taught is generally received by all but the clergy, who think their interest concerned in being made subordinate to the civil power" (VII, 333). Again he expresses his surprise that some even of the episcopal clergy have attacked him, and thinks it can be explained only as a "relic still remaining of popish ambition, lurking in that seditious division and distinction between the power spiritual and civil" (IV, 429). Most significant of all, perhaps, are his remarks in the preface of the *Philosophical Rudiments*, where after saying that he does not "dispute the position of divines, except in those points which strip subjects of their obedience, and shake the foundations of civil government," he goes on to say, "These things I found most bitterly excepted against: That I made the civil powers too large, but this by ecclesiastical persons. That I had utterly taken away liberty of conscience, but this by sectaries. That I had set the princes above the laws, but this by lawyers" (II, xxii–xxiii). In no enumeration of the criticisms brought against his teachings does he mention the principle of absolute sovereignty, nor does he set his doctrine of sovereignty in antithesis to any doctrine except that of divided sovereignty—divided, that is, between the spiritual and temporal power. Locke's doctrine of a sovereignty limited by prior natural rights of those who were its subjects had neither provocation nor justification till after the revolution of 1688 called for some theoretical explanation.

One can hardly, of course, accept Hobbes as an unbiased witness to the way in which his doctrine was received. But Eachard's *Mr. Hobbes's State of Nature Considered* (1696) (a genuinely witty work) gives corroborative evidence that it was not the doctrine of sovereignty which aroused dissent, for he repeatedly states that that was old matter dressed in new form. "Your book called Dominion chiefly consists of such things as have been said these thousands of years." And again, "it might easily be shown how all the rest (so much as is true) is the very same with the old plain Dunstable stuff which commonly occurs in those who treated of Policy and Morality." Aside from the aspersion on human nature contained in Hobbes's doctrine of self-interest, what Eachard objects to is Hobbes's "affected garbs of speech, starched mathematical method, counterfeit appearances of novelty and singularity."[12] How habitually the ideas of the evils of divided sovereignty were in Hobbes's mind appears from a note in the *Rudiments:* "There are certain doctrines wherewith subjects being tainted, they verily believe that obedience may be refused to the city, and that by right they may, nay, ought, to oppose and fight against chief princes and dignitaries. Such are those which, whether directly and openly, or more obscurely and by consequence, require obedience to be given to others besides them to whom the supreme authority is committed. I deny not that, but this reflects on that power which many, living under other government, ascribe to the chief head of the Church of Rome, and also on that which elsewhere, out of that Church, bishops require in theirs to be given to them; and last of all, on that liberty which the lower sort of citizens, under pretence of religion, do challenge to themselves. For what civil war was there ever in the

Christian world, which did not either grow from, or was nourished by this root?" (II, 79n)

As an *argumentum ad hominem* in his own time, it is impossible to overestimate the force of his argument. All Protestants united in declaiming against the claim of the Roman Church to interfere in matters temporal. Yet some of the episcopalian bishops declared that in matters of religious actions, such as rites, appointments, preferments, the church represented God, not man, and had a superior right to obedience. The Presbyterians in general were committed to a dual theory of authority and obedience. Yet all of these ecclesiastical institutions united in reprimanding the fifth monarchy men, Anabaptists, Levellers, etc., who claimed that their personal conscience as enlightened by the indwelling presence of the Holy Spirit was the ultimate source of knowledge of divine law, and hence the rule for obedience. Luther, Calvin, English bishop, and Scotch presbyter alike attacked this doctrine as anarchic and immoral. Hobbes, in effect, points out that all churches are in the same anarchic class, for they all appeal to something other than publicly instituted and proclaimed law.

In connection with the sectaries, it is interesting to note that they expressly cried out for "natural rights derived from Adam and right reason." According to this view, "all men are by nature the sons of Adam, and from him have derived a natural propriety (property), right, and freedom. . . . By natural birth all men are equally free and alike born to like propriety, liberty, and freedom; and as we are delivered of God by the hand of nature into this world, every one with a natural innate freedom and propriety, even so we are to live, every one equally and alike, to enjoy his birthright and privilege."[13] That this anarchic doctrine of the Levellers was wrought by Locke into a stable foundation for a reasonably conservative Whig doctrine, testifies to his altered background and outlook. There is no evidence that Hobbes was influenced by the doctrine, but it is more than a coincidence that he makes a precisely similar notion of natural rights the origin of the war of all upon all, and the basis of demand for absolute sovereignty. If he had this notion in mind in his picture of the state of nature, it adds a piquant irony to his sketch, as well as to his repeated assertions that there was no difference of principle between the sectaries' appeal to the court of private judgment and the doctrines of Papist, Presbyterian, and of such Episcopalians as did not recognize that the authority of the Established Church was by grace of the political sovereign and not by divine right.

Lawson was one of the better tempered and more moderate opponents of royal sovereignty, an episcopalian rector with obvious sympathies with Cromwell. He admits as a "certain truth" that sovereignty is above all civil law, but asserts the supreme legislator "is subject to the superior will of God"—which, of course, was Hobbes's own doctrine. "All the sovereignty's power of making laws, judgments, *etc.*, are from God. . . . Men may give their consent that such a man or such a company of men shall reign, but the power is from God, not them." From this doctrine, it is not a long step to his statement that the true believer in God "may, must within himself, even of laws, so far as they are a rule, and bind him, enquire, examine, and determine whether they are good or evil. Otherwise, he can perform only a blind obedience even to the best; and if he conform unto the unjust, he in obeying man disobeys God, which no good man will do. Romans, xii, 14–15." Subsequently he adds, "Nor does this doctrine anyways prejudice the civil power, nor encourage any man to disobedience and violation of the civil laws, if they be just and good as they ought to be; and the subject hath not only liberty, but a command to examine the laws of his sovereign, and judge within himself and for himself, whether they be not contrary to the laws of God."[14] Yet Lawson joins in the common animadversions upon the leveling sectaries. Moreover, Lawson deplores the disorder and divisions of the time. "Our form of government is confounded by the different opinions of common lawyers, civilians, and divines who agree neither with one another, nor amongst themselves." Nor can the history of England be appealed to as an umpire—as many were doing, for as Lawson, clearer-headed than most, perceived, it shows "only as matter of fact how sometimes the King, Counties, and Barons, sometimes the Commons were predominant and ascendant." And he concludes, "Yet for all this, a free parliament of just, wise, and good men might rectify all this, and *unite the supreme power so miserably divided to the hazard of the state.*"[15] In a situation where a writer sees that the great need is for a unified authority or sovereignty, and yet argues in support of that very principle of private judging of laws which had been a large factor in bringing about the situation he deplores, Hobbes's case almost states itself.

III

A few words are now to be said about another motif in Hobbes's ardent assertion of a unified sovereignty. The part of his doctrine which was not directed against the claim of the churches to obedience was aimed at the claim of the authority of Law set up by the lawyers. To go fully into this matter would require a summary of certain phases of parliamentary history in England, beginning in the time of Elizabeth and becoming highly acute in the reign of James. On the one side were the lawyers and judges, and on the other were the claims of the legislature representing statute law, and of the chancellor representing equity. The king then largely dominated Parliament, and this made the party of the judges against Parliament essentially the popular party of later controversy. In the earlier words of Aristotle, and the later words of the Constitution of Massachusetts, they proclaimed a government "which was a government of laws, not of men."[16]

Consider, for example, such a statement as this of John Milton, arguing against Salmasius: "Power was therefore given to a king by the people, that he might see by the authority committed to him that nothing be done against law, and that he keep our laws and not impose upon us his own. Therefore, there is no regal power but in the courts of the kingdom and by them." And Harrington's constant contention is that only a commonwealth is a government of laws, since law must proceed from will, and will be moved by interest; and only in a commonwealth is the whole will and the whole interest expressed. In a monarchy or oligarchy, the laws are made in the interest of a few, so that what exists is a government of men. Harrington, however, is an innovator in connecting law with legislation rather than with the courts. "Your lawyers, advising you to fit your governments to their laws, are no more to be regarded than your tailor if he should desire you to fit your body to his doublet"—another point of sympathy between him and Hobbes.

It was lawyer's law then which was usually meant—the law of courts, not of legislation. As Figgis says, speaking of the reliance of the popular party upon government by law, "Nor is it of statute law that men are thinking; but of the common law . . . which possesses that mysterious sanctity of prescription which no legislator can bestow. The common law is pictured invested with a halo of dignity, peculiar to the embodiment of deepest principles and to the highest expression of human reason and of the law of nature implanted by God in the heart of man. As yet men are not clear that an Act of Parliament can do more than declare the common law."[17] It is with this doctrine in mind that Hobbes is so insistent that the sovereign is absolved from all law save the moral law—which, as we shall see later, is for him the law of an enlightened hedonism. But Hobbes is not just begging the question. Bacon before him had pointed out many of the defects of common law and the need of codification and systematized revision. The demand for legislative activity was constantly increasing; the Long Parliament in effect restated the common law. Courts of equity had been obliged to assume an extensive activity, and it is not unimportant that the chancellor's court was essentially a royal court and followed the law "of reason," the law "of nature," the law of conscience and of God. Hobbes's essential rationalism was shocked at calling anything law which expressed, as did the common law, merely custom and precedent (III, 91).

Hobbes does away at one sweep with any alleged distinction between written and unwritten law. All law is written, for written *means* published. And as published, it proceeds only from him

(or them) who has authority—power to require obedience. And
that, of course, is the sovereign. "Custom of itself maketh no
laws. Nevertheless, when a sentence has once been given, by
them that judge by their natural reason, . . . it may attain to the
vigor of a law . . . because the sovereign power is supposed
tacitly to have approved such sentence for right. . . . In like
manner those laws that go under the title of *responsa prudentum*,
the opinions of lawyers, are not, therefore, laws because *responsa
prudentum*, but because they are admitted by the sovereign" (IV,
227).[18]

But Hobbes is most explicit in a work, too infrequently made
use of by historians of philosophy, entitled *A Dialogue between a
Philosopher and a Student of the Common Law of England* (VI). This
dialogue opens with an attempt to prove that it is the king's
reason which is the soul even of the common law. He quotes
Coke's saying (and it is to be recalled that Coke had been on the
lawyers' side against King James) that law is reason, although an
artificial reason, got by long study and observation; such a perfec-
tion of reason, however, that "if all the reason that is dispersed
into so many several heads were united into one, yet could he
not make such a law as the law of England is, because by many
successions of ages it hath been fined and refined by an infinite
number of grave and learned men." As against this view, Hobbes
inserts his usual caveat; it was not the succession of lawyers or
judges that made the law, but the succession of kings who created
the judges and who enforced the decisions. "The king's reason,
when it is publicly upon advice and deliberation declared, is that
anima legis, and that *summa ratio*, and that equity . . . which is
all that is the law of England." And even more emphatically:
"There is not amongst men a universal reason agreed upon in
any nation, besides the reason of him that hath the sovereign
power. Yet though his reason be but the reason of one man, yet
it is set up to supply the place of that universal reason which is
expounded to us by our Saviour in the Gospel; and consequently
our King is to us the legislator both of statute law and of common
law" (VI, 14 and 22).[19] Later he suggests that common law and

its lawyers are the chief source of excessive litigation "on account of the variety and repugnancy of judgments of common law," and because "lawyers seek not for their judgments in their own breasts, but in the precedents of former judgments," and also in the liberty they have to scan verbal technicalities (VI, 45). Still later his aversion to reference to mere custom and precedent becomes more marked, and he even goes so far as to say that all courts are courts of equity in principle if not in name (VI, 63) —than which it would be hard to find a doctrine more obnoxious to lawyers—all of which throws light upon the opening sentence of his book, that the study of law is less rational than the study of mathematics, and possibly suggests a slight irony in his reference to the reason of kings as the source of the supreme rationality of common law claimed for it by such a writer as Coke.

IV

When I first became aware of these specific empirical sources for Hobbes's political philosophy, I was inclined to suppose that he had made the latter a necessary part of a deductive system from that inordinate love of formal system to which philosophers are given. And the closing words of the *Leviathan* seem to bear out the impression, when, as if in a relieved tone, he says that having brought to an end his discourse on Civil and Ecclesiastical Government "occasioned by the disorders of the present time," he is now free to "return to my interrupted speculation of bodies natural." Croom Robertson, no mean judge where Hobbes is in question, says "the whole of his political doctrine . . . has little appearance of having been thought out from the fundamental principles of his philosophy. Though connected with an express doctrine of human nature, it doubtless had its main lines fixed when he was still an observer of men and nature, and not yet a mechanical philosopher. In other words, his political theory is explicable mainly from his personal disposition, timorous and worldly, out of sympathy with all the aspirations of his time."[20]

Further study led me, however, to a different position, to the position that Hobbes was satisfied that (even if his ideas had

his search for laws of nature commits himself to the essentially Hobbesian conception that they are "the foundations of all moral and civil knowledge" in such a way as to compel the use of a deductive method. He differs radically as to substance of the fundamental axioms, but agrees as to the form of morals as a science. He "abstains" from theological matters, because he will prove the laws of nature only from reason and experience. He believes that "the foundations of piety and moral philosophy are not shaken, but strengthened by Mathematics and the Natural Philosophy" that depends thereon. In making benevolence, or regard for the happiness of all, his fundamental principle, instead of egoistic regard for private happiness, the influence of Hobbes may be seen in the fact that he, too, starts from Power, but argues that the effective power of man in willing his own happiness is limited to willing it *along with* the happiness of others. And since Hobbes had held that the desire for purely personal good contradicts itself when acted upon, the transformation upon the basis of Power of Hobbes's axiom of self-love into one of benevolence was not difficult.

VI

I do not mean, however, that Hobbes is free from the paradox mentioned. On the contrary, his position is precisely the paradox of attempting to derive by mathematical reasoning the authority of the sovereign to settle arbitrarily all matters of right and wrong, justice and injury, from rational, universal axioms regarding the nature of good and evil. His method of dealing with the paradox takes us to the meaning given by him to natural law, and to his conception of the aim and purpose, or "offices" of sovereignty. Both sides of the matter are worth attention because they reveal a thoroughgoing utilitarianism.

The mistake of so many of Hobbes's critics in thinking that he identified morals with the commands of the sovereign because he identified justice and injustice, right and wrong, with the latter, arises from overlooking the fundamental distinctions which Hobbes draws between *good* and *right*, and between intention and act—or *forum internum* and *forum externum*. Good is simply, to Hobbes, that which pleaseth a man; that which is agreeable to him—which, in turn, means "whatsoever is the object of any man's appetite or desire." It follows, of course, that since men differ in constitution and circumstance from one another, conflict or the state of war ensues; from difference of constitution, because what one man calls good another man finds evil; from circumstance, because when two men find the same object good it ofttimes cannot be shared or mutually possessed. But besides the good of passion or desire of appetite, which is immediately determined by the momentary desire, whatever that may be, there is the good of reason, or rational good. To Hobbes, of course, the rational good does not differ from the sensible good in kind or quality; it is as much the pleasing as is the good of appetite. But it differs in being the object of a survey which includes *time*, instead of being a momentary estimate. For since finding good in present appetite brings a man into conflict with others, it puts his life and possessions in jeopardy; in seeking present pleasure he exposes himself to future evils "which by strict consequence do adhere to the present good," or even to destruction of life. Hence, when a man is in a "quiet mind" he sees the good of present passion to be evil, and is capable of perceiving that his true good lies in a condition of concord or agreement with others—in peace which preserves his body and institutes secure property. "They, therefore, who could not agree concerning a present, do agree concerning a future good; which indeed is a work of reason; for things present are obvious to the sense, things to come to our reason only" (II, 44, 47–48).[27]

Moral laws,[28] laws of nature, are then equivalent to the counsels or precepts of prudence, that is to say, of judgment as to the proper means for attaining the end of a future enduring happiness. The rules of good and evil are the procedures which any man, not perturbed by immediate passion, would perceive to be conducive to his future happiness. Let it be remembered that according to Hobbes all reason (in matters natural as well as moral) is simply a sequence of thoughts directed toward an end which regulates the sequence. Hobbes, then, really believes in laws (or at least counsels) of morality which in their origin are wholly independent of the commands of the sovereign. He ascribes to these all the eulogistic predicates which were scholastically current regarding the laws of nature: they are eternal, immutable, divine, etc. Right reason is the "act of reasoning, that is, the true and peculiar ratiocination of every man concerning those actions of his which may redound to the damage or benefit of his neighbors. . . . I call it true, that is, concluding from true principles rightly framed, because that the whole breach of the laws of nature consists in the false reasoning, or rather folly of those men who see not those duties they are necessarily to perform towards others in order to their own conservation" (II, 16n).[29]

It is not easy to estimate just how sincerely meant were all of Hobbes's professions of piety. I think it may safely be assumed, however, that whether or no he believed in a theological God, he did believe that reasoning was divine, and that there is a sincere piety toward reason in his regarding rational precepts as divine; and that accordingly he believed in some genuine sense that God was reason. There is something besides accommodation in the following language: "Finally, there is no law of natural reason that can be against the law divine: for God Almighty hath given reason to man to be a light unto him. And I hope it is no impiety to think that God Almighty will require a strict account thereof at the day of judgment, as of the instructions which we were to follow in our peregrinations here, notwithstanding the opposition and affronts of supernaturalists nowadays to rational and moral conversation" (IV, 116).

One of the necessary conclusions of such ratiocination on future well-being and conservation is the conclusion that it is not safe for any individual to *act* upon the moral law—which in effect is not to do anything to another which one would not have him do unto us—until he has some guarantee that others will do likewise. A person so acting renders himself exposed to evil from others. Hence suspicion and mistrust, even on the part of one disposed to regard the happiness of others, are inevitable where there is no power or authority which can threaten the evilly minded with such future pains as to give assurance as to their conduct. Hence, it is one of the laws of sound reasoning to enter into a civil state, or to institute a sovereign authority with power to threaten evil doers with evils in return, to such extent as to influence their conduct.[30]

Hence it follows in Hobbes, quite as much as with any of the upholders of the popular theory, that the end or purpose of the state is the "common good." He but insists upon the correlativity of this good with implicit obedience to the commands of a protecting power. To set up any private judgment about the *acts* by which the common good is to be attained is to weaken the protective power, and thereby to introduce insecurity, mutual fear, and discord—all negations to the attaining of that happiness for whose sake the state was instituted. No matter how arbitrary the sovereign's acts, the state is at least better than the anarchy where private judgments as to good (that is to say, immediate appetite and passion) reign.

But there are other checks. The sovereign is himself under the law of nature: that is to say, he is subject to the "sanctions" of utility. As a reasoning creature, he will perceive that his interests as sovereign coincide with the prosperity of the subjects. "The profit of the sovereign and the subject goeth always together"(IV, 164). Hobbes uniformly lays down certain precepts which bind the sovereign's conscience. In his *Leviathan* he develops at length the "Offices of the sovereign." They include equality of taxes, public charity, prevention of idleness, sumptuary laws, equality of justice to all, and the care of instruction. In his earliest writing he mentions all these, and also lays emphasis upon the duty of the civil authority to foster husbandry, fishing, navigation, and the mechanical arts.[31] In his discussion of the need that the state take charge of education, he clearly recognizes the limitations placed upon power to control action through positive commands appealing to fear. *Allegiance to the state is not a matter of positive command, but of moral obligation.* "A civil law that shall forbid rebellion (and such is all resistance to the essential rights of the sovereignty) is not, as a civil law, any obligation but by virtue only of the law of nature that forbiddeth the violation of faith." Hence, its ground has to be diligently and truly taught; it cannot "be maintained by any civil law, or terror of legal punishment" (III, 323–324).[32]

Moreover, there are natural, or utilitarian, checks to the exercise of the power of sovereignty. In the first place, it cannot affect, and (except through education) is not intended to affect inner inclinations or desires, but only acts—which are external. There is always a distinction between the just *man* and a just *act*; the former is one who means to obey the law or to act justly to others, even if by infirmity of power or by reason of circumstance he fail to do so. Even more significant is the check upon despotic action on the part of sovereignty in the mere fact that all acts *cannot* be commanded. "It is necessary that there be infinite cases which are neither commanded nor prohibited, but every man may either do or not do them as he lists himself. . . . As water, inclosed on all hands with banks, stands still and corrupts; having no bounds it spreads too largely, and the more passages it finds the more freely it takes its current; so subjects, if they might do nothing without the commands of the law, would grow dull and unwieldy; if all, they would be dispersed; and the more that is left undetermined by the laws, the more liberty they enjoy. Both extremes are faulty; for laws were not invented to take away, but to direct men's actions; even as nature ordained the banks not to stay, but to guide the course of the stream" (II, 178).[33] The sovereign who attempts too much dictation will provoke rebellion.

This summary account should make it clear that Hobbes deduces the need, the purpose, and the limits of sovereign power from his rationalistic, or utilitarian, premises. Undoubtedly a certain arbitrariness of action on the part of the sovereign is made possible. It is part of the price paid, the cost assumed, in behalf of an infinitely greater return of good. Right and wrong are nothing but what the sovereign commands, but these commands are the means indispensable to procuring good, and hence have a moral or rational sanction and object. To use Hobbes's own words: "In sum all actions and habits are to be esteemed good or evil by their causes and usefulness in reference to the common-wealth" (VI, 220). No franker or more thoroughgoing social utilitarianism could be found.

When we seek for Hobbes's natural historical associates, we should turn not to the upholders of political absolutism for its own sake, but to Jeremy Bentham. They are one in opposition to private opinion, intuition, and *ipse dixitism* as sources of the rules of moral action; they are one in desire to place morals and politics upon a scientific basis; they are one in emphasis upon control of present and private good by reference to future and general good, good being understood by both as pleasure. Their unlikenesses flow from the divergent historic settings in which their ideas were generated. To Hobbes the foe was ecclesiastic interests, the source of divided allegiance and of the assumption of a right of private judgment over against a public law of right and wrong. His remedy was a centralized administrative state. Bentham found the foe in vested economic interests which set private or class happiness above the general good, and which manipulated the machinery of the state in behalf of private ad-vantage. His remedy was a democratizing of government to be obtained by a mass participation in it of individuals, accom-panied by a widening of personal initiative in the choice and pursuit of happiness to the maximum possible limit. To both, however, moral science was one with political science, and was not a theoretical luxury, but social necessity. It was the com-mon fate of both to suffer from a false psychology, from an inadequate conception of human nature. But both are protago-nists of a science of a human nature operating through an art of social control in behalf of a common good. Progress beyond them comes not from a hostile attitude to these conceptions, but from an improved knowledge of human nature.

THE *PHILOSOPHIA PRIMA*
OF THOMAS HOBBES

by Craig Walton

Philosophy, therefore, the child of the world and your own mind, is within yourself; perhaps not fashioned yet, but like the world its father, as it was in the beginning, a thing confused. Do, therefore, as the statuaries do, who, by hewing off that which is superfluous, do not make but find the image.[1]

AMONG HIS REMAINING PAPERS there are some clear indications that Hobbes considered one of his philosophical tasks to be a critique of prevailing philosophies, followed by a fresh grounding of all human inquiries in a natural (non-supernatural) and rational "first philosophy." Despite these intimations, no one has yet examined Hobbes's *philosophia prima* in its own terms. Höffding regarded this philosophy as "the most profound materialistic system of modern times,"[2] but he did not discuss Hobbes's first principles and theory of being. His acute and sympathetic student Frithiof Brandt has made a painstaking exploration of all Hobbes's works from the earliest letters and the "little treatise" until his death in 1679, but Brandt's chief concern was to present Hobbes's contributions to the history of science, especially to "natural philosophy" and the theory of mechanics.[3]

Brandt saw that Hobbes was no "materialist" and considered
him as perhaps the first philosopher of motion, a "motionalist."
Though Brandt referred to Hobbes's metaphysics, as distinguished from his theory of the natural sciences, he did not examine the *philosophia prima.* Since then, the question has been raised
whether Hobbes's philosophy was indeed systematic. Höffding
had already raised some doubts,[4] and since Leo Strauss's book,[5]
discussion has flourished. W. H. Greenleaf[6] recently reviewed
this discussion and so has Arrigo Pacchi.[7] Yet, with the exceptions of Watkins and Riedel,[8] who examined portions of the *philosophia prima,* the analysis of this subject has barely begun.

In what follows I shall explain that Hobbes's scornful critique
of other systems was only the beginning of his greater labor, the
construction of a first philosophy which would avoid the serious
errors of Aristotle and Descartes, but would utilize the best of
their insights. Having achieved this analysis, he was ready to
concentrate on human nature and then on the body politic.

Hobbes begins in Baconian fashion, maintaining that philosophy is both theoretical and practical. It is "the knowledge acquired by reasoning from the manner of the generation of one
thing to the properties, or from the properties to some possible
way of generation of the same; to the end to be able to produce,
as far as matter and human force permit, such effects as human
life requireth."[9]

Hobbes takes geometry very seriously. It provides the concep-
tual equipment for a theory of motion which Aristotle did not
achieve. Euclid erred by bracketing actuality and merely presup-
posing the axioms in "his first element." To Hobbes, first elements should be demonstrated from their foundations in actuality (pt. II, chap. VIII, sec. 22, p. 119). Hobbes thus does not
proceed *de more geometrico,* though he uses "mathematical science"
as a synonym for rational knowledge.

The *Leviathan* opens: "Nature, the art whereby God hath made
and governs the world, is by the *art* of man, as in many other
things, so also in this imitated, that it can make an artificial
animal." *De Corpore* begins with a similar comment: "Imitate the

creation: if you will be a philosopher in good earnest, let your reason move upon the deep of your own cogitations and experience; those things that lie in confusion must be set asunder, distinguished, and every one [then] stamped with its own name set in order." First philosophy is "the natural reason of man, busily flying up and down among the creatures, and bringing back a true report of their order, causes and effects" (I, xiii).[10]

This art of imitating God's creative art is what Hobbes calls "the method of invention." The method of philosophical dialectic or "invention" as a human constructive art to be learned by "imitating" the way God creates and orders nature had been set forth in Peter Ramus's *Dialectique* (1555). By 1650 Ramus's works (chiefly his logic) went through 650 editions, including English translations.[11] Usually writers have emphasized Hobbes's use of "resolutive/analytic" and "compositive/synthetic" methods, derived from the School of Padua (including Galileo, who taught it to Hobbes's friend Harvey). However, Ramus had drawn the same distinction, calling it "analytic/synthetic," and he considered synthesis to be a "genesis" of something "new," as does Hobbes. Unlike Galileo, Hobbes undertakes, as did Ramus, to use his logic as the art whereby men learn to fly "up and down among creatures" and bring back "a true report of *their* order, causes and effects" (my italics). For Hobbes this is not primarily a method either for empirical sciences or for mathematical abstraction but for "first philosophy." His beginning is with the art of names:

To put *genus* and *species* for things, and *definition* for the nature of things, as the writers of *metaphysics* have done, is not right, seeing they be only significations of what we think of the nature of things (*De Corp.*, pt. I, chap. II, sec. 10, p. 21).

There is a certain *philosophia prima*, on which all other philosophy ought to depend; and consisteth principally, in right limiting of the significations of such appellations, or names, as are of all the others the most universal; which limitations serve to avoid ambiguity and equivocation in reasoning; and are commonly called definitions: such as are the definitions of body, time, place, matter, form, essence, subject, substance, accident, power, act, finite, infinite, quantity, quality, motion, action, passion, and divers others, necessary to the explaining of a man's conceptions concerning the nature and generations of bodies (*Leviathan*, p. 440).

First philosophy employs the "method of invention" as do the natural and civil philosophies, but on a different subject matter: first the analysis of some "precognitions" or explication of "simple conceptions." When analyzed, these become the "accidents," and no method is required, for they are "manifest of themselves." They all have one universal cause, which is motion. The method then proceeds to synthesis by way of geometrical generation. On geometry Hobbes would build the effects of one body upon another; this is the "compositive" science of motion.[12]

The first three chapters of part II of *De Corpore* ("The First Grounds of Philosophy") begin with Aristotle's notion of "privation," from which presumably will follow the "matter" and "form" of first philosophy. Like Descartes, Hobbes starts with a "feigned negation." He asks that we imagine the world annihilated and consider ratiocination alone, "sitting still in our closets." Here the focus is on "elements" considered analytically, prior to compounding and construction. He notes that we *could* examine certain basic "precognitions" as if they were "accidents of our minds," or we could imagine them to exist though they do not. What we must do "in the dark" is to examine them only in order to develop "marks" or names by which we can later reckon in regard to questions of existents. Foremost in this analysis is his attack on Descartes's concept of "extension." Descartes's error is that he thought extension could increase continually, whereas in fact there are two issues: (a) Can space be infinite? and (b) Can "magnitude" be multiplied without limit? Hobbes answers "no" to both: it is not a question of what God could do, but of what the names "space" and "magnitude" mean. For Hobbes, "space" means "the phantasm [precognition] of a thing existing without the mind simply." If we ask, "Is the world finite or infinite?" nothing in our minds answers to "world" here. All our imaginings are finite. All we can do is to recognize some concepts as *limiting* concepts. We can set a limit regarding "the least dimensional body," but "the least divisible thing is not to be given." In no case would it make sense to speak of an actual smallest or largest space.

In his attack on the Schoolmen's usage of "spirit" and on Descartes's doctrine of an unextended "thinking substance," Hobbes clarifies his basic term, *body*:

The world (. . . that is, the whole mass of all things that are) is corporeal, that is to say, body; and hath dimensions of magnitude. . . . And because the universe is all, that which is no part of it, is *nothing*; and consequently *nowhere*. Nor does it follow from hence, that spirits are nothing; for they have dimensions, and are therefore really bodies (*Leviathan*, p. 440).[13]

Body signifieth that which filleth, or occupieth some certain room, or imagined place; and dependeth not on the imagination, but is a real part of what we call the *universe*. . . . Because bodies are subject to change, that is to say, to variety of appearance to the senses of living creatures, [they are] called *substance*, that is to say, *subject* to various accidents. . . . *Substance* and *body* signify the same thing; and therefore *substance incorporeal* are words, which . . . destroy one another, as if a man should say, an *incorporeal body* (*Leviathan*, p. 256).

The sense in which a political community can be analyzed and synthesized as a "body politic" received careful consideration in the *Leviathan*. A commonwealth "takes place" literally and is a real body. God, too, Hobbes repeatedly explains to the bishops, is corporeal, whether like *a body* he has determinate magnitude, or whether his magnitude is indeterminate. The "matter" of a body (i.e., there *is* no matter) varies in *activity*. "Spirit is thin, fluid, transparent, invisible body." Its activity is greater than grosser bodies, "its kinds as many as there be kinds of fluids."[14] God is "an infinitely fine spirit, and withal intelligent; [how, therefore, can we doubt that He] can make and change all species and kinds of body as he pleaseth? But I dare not say that this *is* the way by which God Almighty worketh, because it is past my apprehension."[15] Hence first philosophy and the science of bodies cannot extend their causes to God. Theology is faith, not reason.

But Hobbes holds to the tradition that in God we live, and *move,* and have our being. All being takes place and is constituted by activity. *Body* can therefore be used as a better name for *substance.*

Magnitude, place, motion, force, inertia, generation and destruction, essence, form, and matter are all accidents or combinations of accidents. "Accident" means "the manner of our conception of body." An accident is not a part of an actual particular thing, but a universal "part." It is not "in" a thing, but, as Aristotle defined it negatively, it is in its subject "as that it may be away, the subject still remaining." Hobbes puts it more positively than did Aristotle: the accidents cannot perish unless the body also perishes.

Hobbes can now explain how generation and destruction enter into the science of causes. Generation and destruction are not of body from not-body, but of accidents. "Bodies and the accidents under which they appear diversely have this difference, that bodies are things, and not generated; accidents are generated and [are] not things." Magnitude in general is not generated or destroyed, for this might be imagined, but not as occurring in nature.[16] As for Aristotle's *materia prima,* that is "a mere name"; but it might be used for "body in general."[17]

A body is said to *act* when it generates or destroys an accident in another body. "Cause" is "the aggregate of all accidents . . . put together; which when they are all supposed to be present, it cannot be understood but that the effect is produced at the same instant; and if any one of them be wanting, it cannot be understood but that the effect is not produced." That portion of the aggregate which is in the agent is called the "efficient cause," that in the patient "material cause."

However, for a body to be at all, it must be interactive with other bodies. Hence the instantaneity of the causal relation, as given in analysis, means that in actuality causation and production of effects "consist in a certain continual progress: so that as there is a continual mutation in the agent or agents, by the working of other agents upon them, so also the patient, upon which they work, is continually altered and changed" (pt. II, chap. IX, sec. 6, p. 123). "In all action the beginning and cause are taken for the same thing." A beginning is a limit concept: thus to say that motion is the cause of all accidents expresses a limit. Bodies are at once cause and effect; no body is either efficient or else material cause. Any body is both.[18] All four Aristotelian "causes" now become interdependent, perspectival, relational factors in the analysis of "act."

The most neglected feature of Hobbes's innovation is the status he gives to final causes, usually considered to have been banished by him, as they were by Galileo, Descartes, and Spinoza. In order to understand what Hobbes did with teleology we must examine closely chapter X of De Corpore, "Of Power and Act." The phrase "power of the agent" or "active power" has the same meaning with regard to the future as has "efficient cause" with regard to a past act. If an agent body still has all the accidents necessary to be efficient cause on a patient, we may say that it has "power." Similarly, if a patient still has all the accidents necessary to be material cause, it has "passive power." And just as efficient plus material causes together are called the "cause entire," so here the active and passive powers together are called "plenary power" (pt. II, chap. X, sec. 1, pp. 127ff).[19] Active and passive powers exist only when plenary; they cannot act separately. Hobbes is especially emphatic here because his break with classical and Cartesian theories is greatest at this point. "All active power consists in motion" and "is not a certain accident, which differs from all acts, but is, indeed, an act, namely, motion, which is therefore called power, because another act shall be produced by it afterwards." Technically, there are no powers or causes per se; each term is meaningful from a particular standpoint, "power" looking from actuality ahead in time, "cause" looking from actuality backward in time. It takes more than one body to be in act; bodies "are" only when interacting or in motion. Purely passive matter and purely unextended, thinking agents are abstractions from being.

All this leads Hobbes to explain formal and final causes in these terms. Formal and final, like material and efficient "causes," are terms useful a posteriori in singling out certain explanatory factors for study. They are not inherent natural forms or designs.

The culminating "element" in Hobbes's *philosophia prima* is his concept of *conatus* or "endeavor"; it is the *final* synthetic phase of *philosophia prima*, and also the *initial* synthetic phase of natural and civil philosophies.[20] After completing the chapter on "Power and Act" Hobbes wandered afield, for no explained reasons, taking up "identity and difference," "quantity," "analogism," and "strait and crooked, angle and figure." After four intervening chapters of part III, he at last, in chapter XV, arrives at "Of the Nature, Properties and Divers Considerations of Motion and Endeavour." This chapter begins with an apology pointing out that it is a continuation of chapter X, "Of Cause and Effect," which contains "some of the principles of this doctrine that may have been forgotten." It is fairly evident that they had been overlooked by Hobbes himself! He admits that what follows is "new" and "conducing to natural and civil philosophy."[21]

The fifth "recollected" principle which is now "newly" formulated is highly significant. It is an approach to a definition of velocity or momentum: "Motion considered as power, namely that power by which a body moved may in a certain time transmit a certain length." Motion is now considered with regard to the future, to an actual body's capability to undergo motion in a time over a distance: this involves motion interpreted as "power," or, if actually in process, as "act." Such enduring motion is an instance of power and leads Hobbes to his definition of "endeavor": "I define ENDEAVOUR to be motion made in less space and time than can be given; that is, less than can be determined or assigned by exposition or number; that is, motion made through the length of a point, and in an instant of time" (pt. II, chap. XII, p. 2).[22] He immediately emphasizes that he is still dealing with first philosophy, with those universals constructed as conditions of any real body as a whole. There is no question here of "point" as an indivisible thing, like Gassendi's "atom"; "there is no such thing in nature." Rather, "endeavor" refers to the first "small beginnings" or "internal beginnings" of the acts of bodies.[23] "Point" here refers to an "undivided thing" whose quantity is not being considered, rather than to some actual indivisible place. So too with "instant"; it is "an undivided time, not a reference to the existence of a . . . smallest time." In each case the concepts comport with Hobbes's earlier definition of a "limit." Endeavor is the real and rational limit of active power, describing an "active body" rather than the "plenary power." It might be called the irreducible primary category of a theory of actualization. When used in regard to human beings (or, logically, any sensitive being), endeavor is the "initial beginning" which we call desire or appetition.[24]

At this point it should be possible to reweave Hobbes's entire first philosophy, relating it to force, direction, purpose, etc. But Hobbes continues his synthesis by emphasizing that any given endeavor will tend to develop as previously developed motions of the movent have already been moving; or, if there are several movents, as their "concourse determines." This leads him directly to: "HABIT is motion made more easy and ready by custom . . . by perpetual endeavour, or by iterated endeavours in a way differing from that in which the motion proceeded from the beginning, and opposing such endeavours as resist." Such definitions of conservation of energy, and of habit as form-taking conclude Hobbes's first philosophy.

The case for Hobbes's first philosophy as a dialectic whole rests on his logic. In a double sense, this philosophy is imitative of creation. A world in which there is no absolute rest, rest being relative to "equiponderation" of composite endeavors, is in some manner always everywhere active. Where matter and form do not exist in separation, there is no ontological contrast between material and spiritual bodies. Hobbes's *philosophia prima* is not a theory of the natural sciences or of the human sciences; it is a construction by the art of logic of the rational parts, principles, and causes of "bodies in general," explaining how these are constructed by the artifactual talents of God or man. Hobbes in no way avoids the tension between the rational and the real references of his terms; he insists on it, continually reminding his readers that the question of whether this or that term is interpreted rightly or wrongly in a particular context is a problem for the ensuing sciences, natural or civil. He has portrayed a complex intelligible whole with moving parts. Like the sculptors, he claimed, he "found" it in the "rock"; his method of "invention" taught him to imitate the divine art.

Hobbes is clearly not a mechanist. He is emphatic in explaining that all parties to an act are continually changing one another by their interaction and that these changes are conditioning succeeding acts. The more complex bodies make purposive constructions from "within" these natural processes of generation. Classical mechanism, as developed by the Epicureans and adopted by Descartes, Gassendi, and Mersenne in their analysis of nonhuman beings, denied any "activity" to such beings. An initial push from outside the system is merely passed along within the system. Hobbes is, to be sure, an ex post facto determinist; he explains this by his distinction between "cause" and "power." His first philosophy analyzes motion not merely in terms of the natural sciences, but as the "mark" for the "cause" of "universal things," and this theory becomes most explicit in his doctrine of actualization and of processes of generation. Contrary to the mechanists, Hobbes explicitly denies "the void" and the existence of "atoms." And he affirms a providential God. His use of "matter" is classical (correlative of "form") and he has no conception of the existence of matter in general.

What seems significant is that two biologically oriented thinkers, Aristotle and Harvey, are most often acknowledged by Hobbes himself, but are least often credited by his interpreters as sources of Hobbes's theory of motion. Much has been made of Hobbes's remark that civil philosophy, instead of being related to his *philosophia prima* and his natural philosophy, could be developed *ab novo* by anyone who can make a self-examination (pt. II, chap. IV, sec. 7). But what stands out in the case of Hobbes is that self-examination, as well as the logic of "invention," is fundamental to all three: first philosophy, natural philosophy, and civil philosophy. Hobbes, like Ramus before him, was convinced that the art of logic requires searching within one's self and then "imitating" creative art by generating universal forms. He labored long to apply humanist dialectic to the motions and movements of his own time and experience in both natural science and civil affairs. Oakeshott comments eloquently: "Thinking, for Hobbes, was not only conceived as movement, it was felt as movement. Mind is something agile, thoughts are darting, and the language of passion is appropriate to describe their workings." Hobbes described with exceptional *energeia* how he and other natural and civil bodies "live, *move*, and have their being" (*Leviathan*, p. xvi).

SOME PUZZLES IN HOBBES

by Ralph Ross

HOW CAN A MAN be a determinist and yet believe in obligation?
One cannot have an obligation to do something unless he is able
to do it or not to do it. If he cannot do it, it is absurd to say he
is nonetheless obligated to do it; if he must do it because he
cannot do otherwise, he does it as necessity, not as obligation.
Hence genuine obligation rests on freedom. The issue then
becomes: can human action be determined and yet in some way
be free? Hobbes thinks it can, and in chapter XXI of *Leviathan*
says, "*Liberty* and *Necessity* are consistent."

There are easy ways of defending that thesis. A seventeenth-
century thinker could take his cue from Descartes and distinguish body from mind, leaving body determined and mind free,
with no inconsistency, but for Hobbes all is body, even God and
the state. Human behavior, then, is as much determined as are
the motions of the planets. It is still possible to distinguish the
internal from the external in man, the psychological from both
the state of nature and society, and say that man is internally
determined but externally he may be free. This is a reversal of
Descartes. Granted that for Hobbes all is body, he must make
the same distinctions (within body) that other men make, although he may define each part of the distinction differently;

there is still "body" and mind, the environment and the psyche. For Hobbes, a man may do as he wants, but he must want what he wants. Externally, he is free if he may do as he wants, never mind why he wants it. Hobbes defines liberty as the absence of external impediments and again as the absence of opposition, which means external impediments to motion, so he can readily distinguish a necessary will from a free act. Essentially, he does make that distinction. But liberty and necessity, then, are consistent only in not being inconsistent, since they are not in the same context. An examination of his argument (in *Leviathan*, chap. XXI) to establish the consistency of liberty and necessity shows that he wants to predicate both liberty and necessity of nonhuman things as well as of human beings, and that leads to at least two interpretations of what he says.

Water, Hobbes argues, necessarily descends by the channel, but it also has liberty to do so. That follows from his definition of liberty; the water would not descend by the channel if there were external impediments to its motion (internal impediments are a lack of power, not of liberty). Thus liberty and necessity can be predicated at the same time of nonhuman as well as human motion, and seemingly predicated in the same context.

Hobbes makes an analogy between the consistency of liberty with necessity in the descent of water and in "the Actions which men voluntarily doe," yet at first there seems to be no such analogy. Water falls of necessity *because* there is no external impediment to its falling. Man acts of necessity "because every act of mans will, and every desire, and inclination proceedeth from some cause, and that from another cause, in a continual chain." Hobbes says of "the Actions which men voluntarily doe" that "because they proceed from their will, [they] proceed from *liberty.*" If "liberty" means what Hobbes says it means, the absence of "externall Impediments of motion," then it may not seem sufficient that actions proceed from men's will for them to be free; they must also not be hindered. But Hobbes's logic has not failed him here, for he is talking of actions, and actions occur only when they are not hindered.

The apparent failure in the analogy is not due to the definition of liberty but to the use of a single context in the natural instance and of a double context in the human. Water is free and bound in the same context, and bound because it is free. Man is bound in one context, that in which his will is determined by a precedent chain of causes, and free in another, that in which he can act subsequent to willing that act. In the first case, liberty and necessity are consistent; in the second they are independent of each other and so, only in that sense, are not inconsistent. By leaving out constraint, or external impediments, when speaking of human liberty, and speaking only of will, Hobbes makes the analogy to water more plausible, although still not plausible enough.

It is interesting that the will is not mentioned at all in the definition of liberty. But why mention it? We are not likely to try to do what we don't want to do, so it makes little difference if we are stopped from actions we don't intend to perform. Yet it is of both logical and political significance that we may be free to do what we don't want and not free to do what we want, a situation common to despotisms. Hobbes will have none of that and says several times that it is useless to talk of liberty if one doesn't mention the will. In chapter XXI, he defines a free man in the second paragraph: "A Free-Man *is he, that in those things, which by his strength and wit he is able to do, is not hindred to do what he has a will to.*" One is not a free man at all in the absence of external impediments to what he does not want to do (so carefully does Hobbes add to his definition of freedom), but one is not a free man either unless he has the power ("strength and wit") to do what he wants to. A free man has both power and liberty to do his will, a condition that might be called effective freedom.

To return to Hobbes's argument: the relation between liberty and necessity in the instance of water descending is more than consistency. The water flows down if and only if it is not stopped from doing so. Dams, riverbanks, and fallen trees can all stop the flow. There can only be necessity, then, where there is liberty or, put differently, and sounding somewhat whimsical, liberty is a necessary condition of necessity.

In the case of man, the will is bound, but action proceeding from it may be free. Yet the will is still bound if action is bound, too, if we cannot act on the will because of external impediments. Unlike the case of water, then, it is not true that there can only be (human) necessity where there is (human) liberty. When the stream is dammed and it loses its liberty, it is not necessary that it descend, or it would. But the necessity to descend may also be construed as the constant tendency (or disposition, a favorite word of Hobbes) of the water to do so, even when dammed. And the proof is it does so when the dam is removed. Man may have a constant tendency to do some act, even when restrained. And the proof may be that he does it the moment the restraint is removed. Then both water and man are under necessity to do something even when bound, so they cannot do it, and are under the same necessity when free. On this construction, liberty is not a condition for necessity, but is consistent with it. And that is all Hobbes sets out to prove.

On the first construction, a physical object in fact does what it is necessary for it to do, but man may or may not do what necessity dictates; he may only want to. The object is both bound and free in the same context, and bound because it is free. A man is bound whether or not he is free, bound in an internal context and sometimes free in an external one. On the second construction, both object and man are bound whether or not they are free; literally, water is bound by gravitational pull, which is external, but it is easy enough to regard it as internal, and in that case water and man are bound internally and, if free, are free externally. On this second construction, Hobbes's analogy holds. There is still, however, the difficulty with "consistent," but liberty and necessity may coexist, and in that they are not inconsistent with each other.

I think it only fair to accept the second construction and with it the power of Hobbes's analysis. Now, what more can one ask if he still feels uneasy about the congruence of liberty and necessity? No practical difficulty exists because, for all *social* matters, it is irrelevant whether men are psychically free to choose; the great issues about liberty start with the question whether men are free to carry out their choices. Then we can raise further, and vital questions: Should men be free to carry out their choices? If the answer, as seems likely, is that they should be free to carry out some choices and not others, we must ask which choices men should be free to carry out, and why those. The issue soon becomes what is good for man and society, and what is not good.

Yet we cannot assume an all-wise and all-powerful government that tells us which of our choices are good and lets us carry them out, but allows no others. Instead, we ask about the reasons for each of our choices and the probable consequences of acting on them. And this is what more one can ask if he is bothered by the congruence of liberty and necessity (indeed this is why he is bothered), because if the will is determined there is no real choice; "choice" itself is determined. There are no reasons, then, for choices, only causes "in a continuall chain." There are no anticipated consequences of action for our consideration, for those are reasons to choose one way rather than another. There are not even obligations, because a man whose will is bound *must* act to fulfill obligation, or else he *must* act to violate it; he cannot *choose* to do one or the other on principle and with reason.

Whatever force there is in these considerations as they apply to simple determinists, there may be little force in them as they apply to Hobbes, for he makes obligation central to his political thought. In order to test this possibility of his difference, one might look at his treatment of ideas. As a thoroughgoing materialist, he could regard ideas as a product of bodies in motion, but always a product and never a cause. As a good determinist as well as a materialist, he might claim that the ideas a man has are entirely the result of forces external to those ideas, forces that are not themselves ideas. In fact, he does neither. He believes fervently in the power of ideas and writes about them as though they have causal efficacy.

In *De Cive* (II, 1n) Hobbes says, ". . . the whole breach of the laws of nature consists in the false reasoning, or rather folly of those men, who see not those duties they are necessarily to perform towards others in order to their own conservation." The "necessarily" here is a means-end idea, not a determinist one; "or rather folly" does not replace "false reasoning," but merely intensifies it, because this passage is from a note on "right reason." False reasoning, then, is *the* reason for the breach of the laws of nature. And that is coherent with Hobbes's structure, because in it nature's imperative is self-preservation; that we all seek, but knowing how to get it, when it is more than ducking a blow at the head, requires thought. The end is given (determined, if you like), but the means are a product of right reason and are unknown to many. It follows that when men reason wrongly, their means are wrong (except perhaps for good luck, "the secret working of God"), and the end which actually results is destruction, not preservation. Thus our very instincts are flouted by wrong thought and bad ideas. One conclusion is inescapable: although we may be determined to seek survival (the necessity of the will), at least as avoidance of violent death, we are not determined to have it (we may not be free to do as we will, and often lack the power to know how or to do it).

In "The Author's Preface to the Reader" of *De Cive*, Hobbes tells us, ". . . in such matters as are speculated for the exercise of our wits, if any error escapes us, it is without hurt; neither is there any loss, but of time only. But in those things which every man ought to meditate for the steerage of his life, it necessarily happens that not only from errors, but even from ignorance itself, there arise offences, contentions, nay even slaughter itself. . . . How many kings, and those good men too, hath this one error, that a tyrant king might lawfully be put to death, been the slaughter of! How many throats hath this false position cut, that a prince for some causes may by some certain men be deposed! And what bloodshed hath not this erroneous doctrine caused, that kings are not superiors to, but administrators for the multitude! Lastly, how many rebellions hath this opinion been the cause of, which teacheth that the knowledge whether the commands of kings be just or unjust, belongs to private men; and that before they yield obedience, they not only may, but ought to dispute them!"

One can scarcely believe more in the efficacy of ideas than to think they cut throats, even though a hand is needed to hold the knife. If all we will is completely determined, then ideas are among the determinants, and are very strong determinants. But thought and ideas are even more important to Hobbes than they appear in the argument so far. He does not believe man is naturally a political animal; indeed, man is not born fit for society. In *De Cive*, I, 2, the first note makes the full point sharply: ". . . man is made fit for society not by nature, but by education." Whatever else can be said about the passage from nature to society, and Hobbes has so much to say about it, if not for education man would be unfit for society. We must add to the determinants of man's will the skills and ideas, the values and habits of education.

A strange materialist this, a strange mechanist, a strange determinist, when measured by the doctrines to which we give those names today. The genius of the seventeenth century, which produced such extraordinary men, was not reductive and narrowing as the intellectual ethos of the twentieth century is. If Hobbes "reduced" everything to body, body included everything. If we reduce everything to body, there is no spirit, that is, what has been called spirit disappears from existence; when Hobbes reduces everything to body, what had been called spirit still exists, but is now called body, and this is true even of God. For Hobbes there is a change in context, which brings some different ways of viewing things; with many contemporaries there is also an exclusion of things previously supposed to exist.

I am suggesting that it makes no basic difference to Hobbes's politics or even to his psychology that he is a materialist and determinist. He believes, for example, that reason is necessary to check the passions. In chapter XI of *De Homine*, he argues that by nature all men desire what is good for themselves, but that there are real and apparent goods. To this he adds, in chapter

XII, that emotions often interfere with right reasoning. Reason seeks good that lasts and examines consequences. Appetite seizes present good and hinders reason. One might add that the emotions may be inconsistent with survival.

It follows that when reason controls emotion we do what we otherwise would not do or do not what we otherwise would. How, then, can we be determined in all our actions? There is a significant case that education and reason, even if themselves the results of conditioning, set us free from other conditioning. But for Hobbes that makes no difference. If in any particular instance, reason stops a man from doing one thing and makes him do another, that is how he is conditioned. If reason is, however, impeded by emotion and a man chooses an apparent, not a real good, that is how he is conditioned. And we can know in advance of any action that it will be a determined action (whether it is A or non-A), for it can be no other. Under no conditions can this determinist thesis be falsified, nor does it ever lead us to predict one thing rather than another. It does not even bear on moral and political analyses, like those of obligation, contract, covenant, and law. Equally, it makes no particular difference whether all is body or all is spirit.

Within Hobbes's argument, too, he is willing to utter conclusions whose opposites are equally true. In the state of nature, he insists, every man has a right to everything. Of course, he grants that since all men have a right to all things, the rights cancel each other out. Thus it is equally true that in the state of nature, no one has a right to anything. Yet it is important to Hobbes to put it his way, for it fits his system admirably. As he argues it, the right to all things follows from man's one natural right, which is the liberty to use his own power for self-preservation and, consequently, to do anything which, in his judgment, is a good means to that. Because anything may be a means, man has a right to all things. Giving up a right creates obligation, for he must not hinder those who acquire the right. And mutual transferring of right is contract. For Hobbes, then, man in the state of nature must have a right to all, so he can give it away, piecemeal or altogether, thus creating obligation, justice, the commonwealth, and contract.

If man were said to have no rights at all in the state of nature (even the desire to preserve one's life is not a right), then he would have to *acquire* rights through obligation, justice, the commonwealth, and contract. Contract would not be the mutual transferring of rights, but the mutual acquisition of rights. And it could also be the mutual acquisition of things. Instead of my transferring to you my right to a sum of money in return for your transferring to me your right to a commodity, I could acquire the commodity as a return for your acquiring the money. How can I transfer to you my right to a sum of money in return for your transferring to me your right to a commodity when, in the state of nature, you (and everybody else) have as much right to my money as I do, and I (and everybody else) have as much right to your commodity as you do? The answer, I suppose, is that your right to the money in my pocket, although equally valid with mine, doesn't give you possession of the money. A genuine transaction occurs when I transfer my right to money I have, but no transaction takes place if you transfer your right to money that you don't have, that is, nothing can actually be exchanged. The most important matter here seems possession (someone's), rather than rights (everyone's). The same thing is true, of course, if we argue that no one has a right to anything in the state of nature. Why not say, therefore, that we do not transfer rights, but exchange possessions? I acquire the commodity, not a right to it, which I already have as much as you, and in return you acquire money, not a right to it, but the sum itself.

But according to Hobbes I am obligated because I transferred a right, and you, too, are obligated for the same reason. However, instead of being obligated because I have given up a right, I could be obligated because I have made a promise. Why would I make a promise that obligates me? For some benefit I foresee, perhaps. After all, why would I give up a right, on Hobbes's account? For just that reason, he says, and adds that it is a voluntary act. And my promise, too, which could be the basis of obligation, is a voluntary act.

The point is that the same kind of system could be constructed on the assumption (a much more realistic one, I think) that men have no rights by nature, but acquire them in society. Yet Hobbes does it the other way. It is as if the analogy were to commerce and commercial contracts. Men spend and exchange rights as they spend and exchange money and commodities.

To continue, for the moment, with Hobbes's determinism and the use of statements that could easily be their opposites. What we desire is called good, what we shun evil. Appetite and aversion are all that count, and nothing is good in itself, but good for someone. Because appetite and aversion are determined for each of us, it follows that good and evil are determined in each case and differ from man to man. But, as I have already said, some good is real and some only apparent, so one's reason must intervene to choose his real good in any particular instance (*De Homine*, XI, 5). Although the words are different, this is a distinction between the desired and the desirable, and it would be apt and intelligible to call the desirable, namely, what is chosen after reflection, good. But more important, Hobbes's insistence that desire and aversion are bound is no longer significant. In *De Homine* (XI, 2) he makes his point about bondage simply and strongly: "When desiring, one can, in truth be free to *act*; one cannot, however, be free to *desire.*" Yet all this makes no difference because of the need for reason in choosing *real* good. One can call reason, too, bound, but not by the same causal chain as desire and aversion, and their intersection corrects and qualifies the result of the causal chain leading to apparent good and evil.

Further, freedom in desire and aversion (and we should know what that freedom would mean even if it doesn't exist) is not the absence of external impediments, nor is bondage in desire and aversion the presence of external impediments. There are no such impediments possible. In the paragraph just cited, Hobbes says: "Neither our appetite nor our aversion causeth us to desire or shun this or that; that is, we do not desire because we will. For will itself is an appetite; and we do not shun something because we will not do it, but because now appetite, then aversion, is generated by those things desired or shunned, and a preconception of future pleasure and displeasure necessarily follows from those same objects." We respond to things real or imagined in desire or aversion because of what they are and what we are, both the result of causal chains. One simply likes or dislikes lager beer, and in that sense he is bound (although, of course, in cultivating taste he changes response). Thus freedom and bondage have one meaning when predicated of the will and another meaning when predicated of action. But the bondage of the will is overcome in reflection, even if we want to call reflection bound, too.

Good and evil are natural responses, modified by reflection on consequences to yield real good (and understand real evil, one may presume); justice and injustice, right and wrong cannot be predicated of anything in the state of nature. "They are qualities, that relate to men in Society, not in Solitude." Yet to hinder those to whom a right is granted from using it is injustice. The third law of nature, "That men performe their covenants made," is the font and source of justice: injustice is defined as not performing a covenant. Covenants can be made in the state of nature, and so justice and injustice do occur in the state of nature. This sounds like a contradiction but is only a paradox whose resolution, briefly, is that in the state of nature we are bound in conscience to the laws of nature, bound, that is, "to a desire they should take place," but not always bound to act on them. That comes only in the commonwealth, where the laws of nature become civil laws.

When that does happen, when the laws of nature become civil laws by enactment of the sovereign, we are obligated to obey them in action, for we are obligated to obey the sovereign. But in this particular case, I think, our obligation runs deeper than our obligation to pay taxes, abide by traffic laws, or do whatever else the sovereign commands. We are also obligated to accept the laws of nature in conscience, because they are moral. There is a double obligation, then, to the laws of nature when they become laws of the state, an obligation that is both natural and social, moral and political. In the state of nature, the laws of nature (which are the conclusions of right reason, rather than law, except insofar as God commands them) are already a code of morals, immutable and eternal, based on man's fundamental drive for survival, which is basically invariant. Yet Hobbes does not enjoin us to behave morally when other men do not, for thus we would destroy, not preserve ourselves, and the laws of nature are a code of morals grounded in self-preservation. It should follow that if we remove the ground, we remove the morality of the laws of nature. Hobbes speaks of "the ground of all Lawes of Nature," but one could as easily speak of the end.

Let me examine some of this in more detail, so the puzzles in it are more apparent. The laws of nature are "dictates of reason" which tend to self-preservation; they can be thought of as means to the end of preserving ourselves. But unless most (or many, or concerned) men obey them, for whatever reason, morality, habit, fear of personal reprisal or judicial punishment, they will not work. They will not be means to the end we properly and naturally desire. And in consequence they will not constitute a moral code, because the other laws of nature follow from the first law (*Leviathan*, chap. XIV), which states: "*Seek Peace, and follow it.*" This first law itself is contained in a prior "precept, or generall rule of Reason, *that every man ought to endeavour Peace, as farre as he has hope of obtaining it.*" Hobbes's definition of a law of nature makes the point more clearly: "A Law of Nature, (Lex Naturalis,) is a Precept, or generall Rule, found out by Reason, by which a man is forbidden to do, that, which is destructive of his life, or taketh away the means of preserving the same; and to omit, that, by which he thinketh it may be best preserved." All laws of nature, then, state the means of preserving and destroying life, and enjoin the one while forbidding the other.

The "precept, or generall rule of Reason," which contains the first law of nature, but states it more elaborately, tells every man to "*endeavour Peace, as farre as he has hope of obtaining it,*" but does not urge that endeavor beyond our hope of obtaining it. Indeed, the same precept continues, "and when he cannot obtain it, that he may seek, and use, all helps, and advantages of Warre." The laws of nature, as Hobbes states them, are not in one sense a moral code except insofar as they actually preserve life if we act on them, because the aim of a moral code is to preserve life. Put differently, the laws of nature are a formal moral code which is effective only under particular material conditions, and not under others. Those laws are binding morally (and what is a moral code without an "ought") when they are likely to be effective and not when they are likely to be ineffective. Yet they are our one chance of obtaining our end, so our great task becomes creating and maintaining the material conditions which may make the code effective. And those conditions can be summarized as a commonwealth.

In order that they may live in a civilized way, with agriculture, navigation, trade, architecture, science, arts, and letters, men need a commonwealth; above all, they need it to minimize the danger of violent death, and for that they need morality. In the commonwealth, as I have suggested, they are doubly bound by the laws of nature, which are also civil laws, and which are fully moral, having both the formal and the material conditions of morality. But in the state of nature the status of those laws seems equivocal. They are the morals we need and want, but we must remember that in the state of nature nothing can be unjust; justice and injustice, right and wrong are not even predicates. Hobbes could hardly say this more strongly than he does at the end of chapter XIII of *Leviathan*, but in chapter XV he speaks of just and unjust men, and of just and unjust actions. This is still in part I, "Of Man," not in part II, "Of Common-Wealth," and Hobbes makes no qualification about just and unjust having meaning here only when there is a common power above all men.

The clearest case of a covenant that is obligatory "in the condition of meer Nature" is one entered into by fear. If I covenant to pay a ransom or service to an enemy in return for my life, I

am obligated to pay. In a commonwealth the civil law may intervene; in nature only accident can. Apart from that instance,
Hobbes seems to suggest things that might help us fulfill our
covenants. "The force of Words, being . . . too weak to hold men
to the performance of their covenants; there are in mans nature,
but two imaginable helps to strengthen it. And those are either
a Feare of the consequence of breaking their word; or a Glory,
or Pride in appearing not to need to breake it." It turns out that
these are not to be relied on, except perhaps for fear of God, and
finally one doubts whether that helps very much. These helps
are "imaginable" helps, and no more. Even the passage that
seems unequivocal to some commentators is not so. In *Leviathan*,
XV, Hobbes writes: "That which gives to humane actions the
relish of justice is a certain Noblenesse or Gallantnesse of courage, (rarely found,) by which a man scorns to be beholding for
the contentment of his life, to fraud, or breach of promise." Some
few noble men, it might seem, will perform their covenants
courageously, whatever happens to them. Yet this nobleness or
gallantness of courage sounds like the glory or pride of the passage previously quoted, of which Hobbes says, "This latter is a
Generosity too rarely found to be presumed on." There are a
very few such exceptional men, Hobbes may believe, but they
make no real difference in the conduct of affairs in the state of
nature.

I think commentators on Hobbes have refused to call all this
a maze of contradiction and equivocation because it is too obviously such for a man of Hobbes's great powers and almost un-
believable care. Of course, he occasionally slips, but the logic of
his argument is usually so compelling and his insights so percep-
tive and beautifully tailored to the larger structure that a mass
of gross contradictions simply cannot be attributed to him. It
may be our unsettled times that have brought so many writers
to a new appraisal of Hobbes. Perhaps he offers more promise
of stability than do other writers, perhaps it is becoming apparent how many widely accepted ideas we owe to him and how he
avoided a number of our errors in dealing with those ideas. What-

ever the reasons for the Hobbes revival, the puzzles I have set out have led to strong partisan statements: there is obligation in the state of nature, there is no obligation in the state of nature; there is justice in nature, there is no justice in nature; the laws of nature create obligation, they do not create obligation; and so on.

Hobbes seems at times to cause these disputes by a quality of his rhetoric, in which something is stated firmly and then taken away. A good example, in addition to some passages already discussed, occurs in chapter XV of *Leviathan*. In the next to last paragraph, Hobbes extols the laws of nature, saying, ". . . the true Doctrine of the Lawes of Nature, is the true Moral Philosophie." Yet the last paragraph starts: "These dictates of Reason, men use to call by the name of Lawes; but improperly: for they are but Conclusions, or Theorems concerning what conduceth to the conservation and defence of themselves." Among the men who used to call these dictates of reason by the name of laws is Hobbes himself, a few lines above, and the true moral philosophy turns out to be a set of conclusions about what helps in self-preservation. The new reader may be forgiven if he is startled, and the scholar if he accepts one or the other of Hobbes's assertions, but not both.

A rhetorical device that Hobbes often employs is a use of the language of a tradition, sometimes weighed down by scholarship about Greek and Latin words and roots, or ancient history, and then a sudden switch to what it all means in his own more hardheaded terms. Hobbes has called his dictates of reason natural laws for many pages before the passage cited and has spoken of moral philosophy with proper respect. Then in his last brief paragraph here he tells what that amounts to. What it amounts to does not belittle what was said before, but makes it more precise. The laws of nature (a traditional name) are the true moral philosophy, but because, as he also says in the last paragraph, "Law, properly is the word of him, that by right hath command over others," the laws of nature are not properly called laws at all, except as God commands them, and moral philosophy, as he has constantly argued, has its ground, or end, in self-preservation and is rationally derived from that ground or aimed toward that end.

Another rhetorical device in Hobbes is stating a case as directly and unequivocally as possible to make an immediate impact on the reader. Once the impact has been made, however, the qualifications follow. If the qualifications meet all the objections that came to the reader's mind when he recovered from the shock of the first statement, he may be persuaded. But the qualifications take much away from what Hobbes said originally, and may even convert it into something else. When the qualifications do not follow at once on a statement, but come later, sometimes much later, Hobbes seems inconsistent even when he is not. Putting the qualifications later is a gain in dramatic impact, and it allows Hobbes to pursue a line of argument without the eddies and backwaters that muddy it, but it also involves the risk that the qualifications may seem to destroy the statement and much of the argument. There are special stylistic matters that have to be understood when we read any major philosopher (and some minor ones); otherwise we will not grasp his full sense. And these are among Hobbes's favorite devices.

As for the passages in which justice and injustice have no place in the state of nature, and the many passages in which they do, the most likely resolution of these seeming contradictions is what I have suggested briefly. We are just when we accept our obligations in all conscience and "endeavour Peace," which encompasses all the laws of nature Hobbes discusses, and of course includes performing our covenants, as far as we have hope of obtaining peace. Self-preservation is included in peace, so we are enjoined to endeavor to fulfill our obligations insofar as they do not lead to our destruction. But it is not necessary in the state of nature that we actually perform in order that we be just; wanting to perform and seriously trying (within the limits stated) are enough.

Confusion about all this is created by Hobbes's second rhetorical device. After saying there is neither justice nor injustice in nature, he nevertheless writes about what is somehow just and unjust for two chapters, and only at that point makes his qualification, the distinction between justice in conscience, *in foro interno*, and justice in action, *in foro externo*. Then he goes on to say that a man is just in the state of nature if he really endeavors to do what he ought (i.e., fulfill the laws of nature). But if he really endeavors to do it, one supposes, he might succeed, and thus destroy himself. It is in still another passage that the further qualification is made, "as farre as he has hope of obtaining it." Hobbes's rhetorical device is dramatically successful here, I think, but the distance between statement and qualification demands patience and a lengthy suspension of disbelief.

It may still seem that Hobbes does not square his initial denial that justice and injustice have any place at all in the state of nature with his later assertion that justice and injustice do exist in nature, although only *in foro interno*. I think the proper response to this puzzle is that the initial statement meant justice and injustice as we know them in the commonwealth, i.e., *in foro externo*. That is reasonable enough, because justice and injustice as we normally think of them are invariably bound up with action; it is for the state of nature only that we must make the special case that thought and conscience, without action, may be sufficient for a man to be called just. And, rhetorically, if that had been intimated in the initial statement it would have lessened its power. The great prose of *Leviathan* makes far more difficulties than the more workmanlike manner of *De Cive*.

But we have not yet explained why Hobbes wrote of rights and other matters in an unnecessarily difficult way (or so it seems to me), when he could have reached essentially the same conclusions much more simply. He does it, I think, for the same reason that he introduces a mechanist-determinist philosophy into his discussion of human liberty and bondage, insisting on an analogy to the flow of water, which really does nothing to further his argument. Hobbes was possessed by the belief that the whole universe was related and could be explained in a single way. The unity of knowledge, based on science, a cornerstone of Diderot's eighteenth-century *Encyclopédie*, was first a seventeenth-century belief, of which Hobbes was a great pioneer, perhaps *the* great pioneer. That doctrine posits a coherent world.

What is the cement that makes a world coherent, that keeps it of one piece? First, monism; and Hobbes was a materialistic monist. Second, a necessary connection of all parts; and that Hobbes provided by determinism. The world is ruled by a vast necessity in which God, too, plays his part. Hobbes keeps to his thesis, as in his treatment of good and evil, but when he has to qualify it to make good sense, he does, as in the role of reason in finding real good. Then the qualification has to fit the basic thesis, and at this point it no longer makes any difference whether that thesis is true or false. The important argument has been stated; the Procrustean bed need not be made.

No thinker in our own age, perhaps, is so ambitious as Hobbes. We are given more to criticism, small-scale analysis, and occasional hypothesis than to large construction, especially of an all-embracing system of thought. We have decided, I think, that politics and ethics, which Hobbes thought demonstrable a priori (*De Homine*, chap. X), cannot be derived from physics or metaphysics. We too easily forget the enchantment of a vision of total explanation, the ambition to be the man who understood the system of the universe, compared to whom Alexander and Napoleon were petty, unimaginative men. Our scale of possibility is so much smaller, and we are so sure our scale is right, that the introduction of the considerations of systematic philosophy into an argument often confuses us.

Too often, alas, we live with the rigidities of recent thought, which makes us scorn anything to the contrary. A recent article is a good example of how we may make ourselves incapable of understanding Hobbes because our own beliefs make sympathetic reading impossible. Richard S. Peters and Henri Tajfel wrote a paper, "Hobbes and Hull: Metaphysicians of Behavior" (published in *Hobbes and Rousseau*, ed. Maurice Cranston and Richard S. Peters, 1972), comparing Hobbes with the American psychologist Clark Hull. Hull is quoted (p. 183) as saying that the methods of natural science will enable us to "deduce" the behavior of organisms, including the making of moral judgments. The authors comment, "Now it is understandable that Hobbes should also have shared this methodological pipe-dream; for he lived before Hume and Kant had shown the logical impossibility of deducing statements about what ought to be from statements about what is the case." Hull, of course, has no such excuse.

Instead of being explained by his time, Hobbes is thus condemned for living when he did. Instead of being used so we can learn from him (and his marvelous insights into morality, for instance, have barely been tapped), Hobbes is chided for not being like us. The value of studying a historical figure is diminished by such contemporary arrogance, and the very idea of history is lost. Fortunately, Hobbes will survive all this, as he has survived so much misrepresentation in the past.

HOBBES ON THE GENERATION
OF A PUBLIC PERSON

by Theodore Waldman

IN THIS BRIEF STUDY of an aspect of Hobbes's philosophy I shall
concentrate on his notions of power, the laws of nature, and the
generation of a public person. Previously[1] I had pointed out that
his examination of the liberty of natural bodies rested upon a
rejection of the possibility of knowing supernatural bodies (e.g.,
God or soul), the acceptance of a mitigated or constructive skepticism regarding our knowledge of the motion of natural bodies—a
concept recently examined by R. H. Popkin in his studies of
seventeenth-century skepticism—and the application to human
behavior of Galileo's conjecture concerning the motion of bodies
when all external impediments are removed. Liberty is a crucial
concept in the development of Hobbes's political philosophy
also, but is not to be confused with that of power. What I hope
to develop is a commentary upon Hobbes in which his concepts
of liberty and power regarding the individual are understood as
fundamental to his notion of authorized power and civil liberty
in the generation of a public person. I shall also emphasize that
those who see in Hobbes's political philosophy the application
of a narrow view of self-love (selfish egoism) misunderstand him.
The sacrificial acts and enlightened self-interest (altruistic motivation) incumbent upon those who seek peace will be under-

scored, the responsibilities of the public person (sovereign commonwealth) made clear, and the basic value of social or communal goods in his system stressed.

I

In his Epistle Dedicatory to the Earl of Devonshire prefacing the English translation of *De Corpore* Hobbes paid tribute to his friend William Harvey as the founder of a new science. He stated: ". . . the science of *man's body*, the most profitable part of natural science, was first discovered with admirable sagacity by our countryman Doctor Harvey, principal Physician to King James and King Charles, in his books of the *Motion of the Blood,* and of the *Generation of Living Creatures*; who is the only man I know, that conquering envy, hath established a new doctrine in his life-time. Before these, there was nothing certain in natural philosophy but every man's experiments to himself. . . ."[2] Harvey and Hobbes were friends, close enough that when the former died, "he left his old friend Mr. Thomas Hobbes 10 pounds as a token of his Love."[3] Harvey not only had demonstrated the motion of the heart and circulation of the blood, correcting the views of Galen and instituting a revolution in medical science, but in his work often used metaphorical references that likened the heart and blood to sovereign and commonwealth or sun and world.[4] In his dedication to King Charles I in 1628 he states:

The heart of animals is the foundation of their life, the sovereign of everything within them, the sun of their microcosm, that upon which all growth depends, from which all power proceeds. The King, in like manner, is the foundation of his kingdom, the sun of the world around him, the heart of the republic, the fountain whence all power, all grace doth flow. . . . many things in a King are after the patterns of the heart. . . . Here, at all events, best of Princes, placed as you are on the pinnacle of human affairs, you may at once contemplate the prime mover in the body of man, and the emblem of your own sovereign power.[5]

Later, in speaking of the circulation of the blood, he describes it as returning

. . . to its sovereign the heart, as if to its source, or to the inmost home of the body . . . it renews its fluidity, natural heat, and becomes powerful, fervid, a kind of treasury of life . . .

The heart, consequently, is the beginning of life; the sun of the microcosm, even as the sun in his turn might well be designated the heart of the world; for it is the heart by whose virtue and pulse the blood is moved, perfected, and made nutrient, and is preserved from corruption and coagulation; it is the household divinity which, discharging its function, nourishes, cherishes, quickens the whole body, and is indeed the foundation of life, the source of all action.[6]

Harvey also stresses the destructive consequences that occur to man's body and to his passions when the heart no longer functions properly. Health may be regained with a sound heart, but apparently not without one. He points out:

. . . if the heart be unaffected, life and health may be restored to almost all the other parts of the body; but if the heart be chilled, or smitten with any serious disease, it seems matter of necessity that the whole animal fabric should suffer and fall into decay. When the source is corrupted, there is nothing, as Aristotle says, which can be of service either to it or aught that depends on it. And hence, by the way, it may perchance be why grief, and love, and envy, and anxiety, and all affections of the mind of a similar kind are accompanied with emaciation and decay. . . . For every affection of the mind that is attended with either pain or pleasure, hope or fear, is the cause of an agitation whose influence extends to the heart . . . impairing all nutrition in its source and abating the powers at large. . . .[7]

Although Harvey does not carry his analogy between heart and sovereign into this discussion, nonetheless one might do so for him, as in fact, I believe, Hobbes did. When the health of the commonwealth is affected and its sovereign is chilled or smitten, then the decay of the public person and its destruction follow. The power of the public person makes possible its action; no power, no action. But at this point remembering Harvey's words let us turn to Hobbes to see his development of these concepts and their use in his political philosophy.

II

In discussing liberty Hobbes had held that external impediment to a body in motion could be applied no less to irrational and inanimate creatures than to rational ones. He, of course, noted also that it applied to a river (inanimate creature?) moving within its banks. In what seems to me a profound insight when speaking of internal rather than external impediments to motion Hobbes stated, ". . . we use not to say; it wants the liberty; but the power to move; as when a stone lieth still, or a man is fastened to his bed by sickness" (III, 196). His view emphasizes the internal conditions, that which he calls *vital motions* (III, 38),[8] (flow of blood, pulse, nutrition, etc.), which make possible an animal body's motion. In this he reads much like Harvey. Internal impediments to internal motions lessen the power of the body so that its action may be impaired. The vital motions also make possible voluntary motion in a human body (Hobbes calls it "animal motion"); voluntary motion properly relates to the liberty a body has in its movement, for external impediment may hinder or prevent that body (animal body) from moving when it decides to move. Voluntary motion is not properly attributed to inanimate bodies although their movement too may be hindered or interfered with by external impediments.

If we take Hobbes's concept of liberty as applied to human bodies in motion as they endeavor to approach that which they desire (or toward that for which they have an appetite) or to depart from that to which they have an aversion, then they are most at liberty which have least external impediments. If they are incapable of moving because of some internal impediment, then we would state that they are powerless; if capable, then they have the power to move. To put it another way, one may be at liberty to move (no external impediments) but be powerless ("internally" unable for many reasons) or not at liberty to move (external impediments, e.g., chains) and have the power to move (is internally capable of moving). Power, for Hobbes, also generally refers to those means that a man has to achieve some future apparent good; it is either original (internal—be it bodily or mental) or instrumental (something he or a group of men fashion) (III, 74).

As is well known Hobbes considers men competing for those goods that are necessary to life in a condition in which they are without a government or commonwealth. He calls this condition "the state of nature." In it there are external impediments and internal ills to men who would freely move, seeking to increase their vital motion. Nature does not supply sufficiently for their wants, and in this state of nature (perhaps Hobbes's view of nature after the fall of man), they compete for goods, fear one another, and seek the bubble reputation—a vanity in which they demand respect and submission from their fellowmen. Thus in competition, diffidence, and vainglory Hobbes finds passions that lead us to war. The difficulties in satisfying wants have concomitant effects within the individual: to be finite is not to be omnipotent. Naturally men have a right to use their capacities to preserve their lives; the presence and use of these capacities are their power and, as noted, are conditional upon both external impediments (hence the liberty a man has to use his power) and internal calm or health. It is also obvious that external impediments may lead to curtailment of power. Fear is internal but may be generated by external objects. Man's natural right is understood descriptively; it is found in the picture of a creature pursuing his interests, meeting opposition, either overcoming it or being overcome by it, fearing or strutting depending upon circumstances. For Hobbes it is also the picture of nations competing with one another for the goods of the earth; it is also the picture of individuals within a nation waging civil war. In every case it is a picture of men or nations using prudence as a guide or behaving passionately to secure goods; all this without a common earthly judge or authority over them. (Common, in the sense that that judge or authority would be recognized by the individuals who agree to abide by his or its decision.)

Returning to our examination of an individual who is at liberty, we recall that it is his right of nature to seek future apparent goods to preserve his life—that is the way he acts. In so acting, however, he and others engage in a state of war which is identified with the state of nature. By acting voluntarily as individuals they are not able to achieve that purpose toward which their acts were directed. In fact, the very opposite, paradoxically, occurs. They increase their external impediments and decrease their power, both of which make the accretion of future apparent goods dubious and the heightening of vital motion perilous. As Hobbes magnificently puts it: "and the life of man [is] solitary, poor, nasty, brutish, and short" (III, 113). For, as noted, both his power, which is an expression of his internal condition, is lost and his liberty is curtailed. Fear may make men powerless (unstable, lacking self-control, not at peace, etc.) and their voluntary motion chaotic (i.e., their behavior erratic and imprudent). In order for a man ideally to be author of his actions (act with authority) he must be at peace with himself (stable, "powerful"); in being author of his action he has the potentiality of using his power with maximum efficiency; that is, he is able to procure and secure those future apparent goods that he desires. The absence of external impediments (his liberty) obviously enhances this.

Let us examine this in more detail. In speaking of men as men, and not in a commonwealth, or perhaps better, in speaking of the individual man as such, we describe a creature who is a self-contained person by nature. He, of course, is not self-sufficient. If we take a multitude of individuals who compete for the goods of nature in order to survive, we find, as we also noted, that owing to the niggardliness of nature and the diffidence, competitiveness, and vainglory of men that multitude inevitably enters into or is within a state of war. Referring to men in a multitude as without anything to bind them together (i.e., unite them), without a common authority, Hobbes holds that that is their natural (nonconventional or nonartificial) condition and calls it "the state of nature." Since in that state we find that the conditions leading to war or war itself is present, Hobbes also calls it "the state of war." (For Hobbes recognizes that a cold war is yet war.) Nonetheless in that state men also have the potentiality to make peace. Their ability to learn from experience and imaginatively project that knowledge into the future in considering causes and consequences of actions, along with a passionate desire of those things necessary to commodious living (denied them in war), a passionate fear of death (increased greatly in war), and a passionate hope to use those tools industriously which make a commodious life probable (a probability decreased by war) all aid them in making peace. Peace, the opposite of war, provides the possibility of uniting liberty and power most advantageously.

Since Hobbes recognizes that men as created (naturally) lose both power and liberty in war and since power and liberty are necessary to their preservation, Hobbes seeks that which reason and the passions might offer (if at all) to end war and "reunite" liberty and power. Now, of course, it is the very fact that men have power and liberty that they have the ability to move and do move in a certain direction depending upon external impediments and inevitably are able to and do get into war and so lose their power and liberty. A paradox of life, as we noted. This "paradox" has important ramifications for Hobbes's political theory. For, in a very real sense, it points up the impossibility of self-government. Obviously this is not the full sense of the term as used today, but it bears an important resemblance to it. Men, on their own, pursuing those goods which not only make life possible but make a felicitous life capable of realization, are not able to control themselves sufficiently (govern themselves) to avoid war. War lessens or ends the prospect of living as well as living well. As we shall see, since men cannot gain those consequences that enable them to live a good life when they pursue them on their own initiative, they must seek some other way to achieve that life.

III

Hobbes in his long life not only had "seen" England develop as a major power under Elizabeth I but had witnessed its execution of its king, Charles I, and its establishment of the Protectorate under Cromwell by the time or shortly after *Leviathan* was published. He had lived through a state of war in which men were without a common authority over them. He had listened to claim and counterclaim, heard each justified to the exclusion of the other, had experienced the frustration that ensues when neither claimant will abide by the decision of a common authority. This is especially true in a civil war in which that very authority is both under attack and defended by different factions of one people. The events that he had observed in Britain, had read about and translated in Thucydides, and had studied in Cicero and Livy, events concerning the antecedents and consequences of war, formed the basis for his philosophical reflections about and recommendations for the generation and continuation of the body politic. Thucydides's description of the claims and counterclaims of Athens and Sparta and their allies that led to the Peloponnesian War was exactly what Hobbes meant by the state of nature and war among nations.

The problem for Hobbes was not the causes and consequences of rebellion, albeit he was surrounded by events that might be so studied; rather was it the generation of a commonwealth or the establishment of peace. He had seen in the failure of men or nations to maintain peace the breakdown of the proper relationship between power and liberty. Power in the commonwealth is for Hobbes authority; both terms are heavy with connotations and hence not simple in their denotation. When he states, "For in a way beset with those that contend, on the one side for too great liberty, and on the other side for too much authority, 'tis hard to pass between the point of both unwounded" (III, Epistle Dedicatory to Mr. Francis Godolphin), it is power and liberty that he is contrasting. It is in a man's use of his power that he is an author. It is the union of power by men that constitutes a commonwealth. Since men had failed as a multitude (an accidental collection of private persons) to achieve their needs, had failed as authors, we noted that another kind of attempt was needed.

Spiritually men are or have been united under God; their union depends upon their covenant (old or new) or consent to

submit to him. The blessings of the covenant, that their days may
be long upon the land which the Lord, their God, giveth them,
are the blessings of peace. The signs of that covenant are either
circumcision or baptism. In that union under God is created a
new person, the person of the chosen or the elect as well as a new
nation. For Hobbes the relation that men have to God is established by faith, not knowledge (except for the first cause argument which only remotely is related to belief in God), as we
noted in our earlier discussion of liberty. Their union is tied up
with faith, revelation, hope within this world now and in the
future, love, and worship. God's authority or power does not rest
upon their consent, but their submission to him does. It is God
who empowers or authorizes them.

Hobbes finds in this, I believe, the basis for the formation of
a union of men on earth dedicated to peace and the securing of
a contented life thereby, notwithstanding the insecurity, impon-
derables, and ill luck that men encounter here. In that union, as
we shall see, Hobbes, as it were, reverses the covenant that ob-
tains under God. In generating a public person (that mortal god
Leviathan) men empower or authorize it. In common with the
divine covenant they submit also, but to a mortal one. He sees
in the union of men a hope for peace and the possibility through
enhanced capabilities to secure goods that under the best of circumstances men could not secure alone. The goods that he discusses in the paragraph containing the aforementioned statement
of the condition of the life of man in the state of nature are the
goods over which men in society may aspire. It is worthwhile
stating the entire paragraph for it also provides the kernel of an
argument against those who see in Hobbes an individualist who
looks upon the commonwealth as a necessary evil.

Whatsoever therefore is consequent to a time of war, where
every man is enemy to every man; the same is consequent to the
time wherein men live without other security, than what their
own strength, and their own invention shall furnish them withal.
In such condition, there is no place for industry; because the fruit
thereof is uncertain; and consequently no culture of the earth;

no navigation, nor use of the commodities that may be imported by sea; no commodious building; no instruments of moving, and removing, such things as require much force; no knowledge of the face of the earth; no account of time; no arts; no letters; no society; and which is worst of all continual fear, and danger of violent death; and the life of man, solitary, poor, nasty, brutish, and short (III, 113).

It is clear that Hobbes is not arguing merely for bare preservation. It is obvious, that without life and with continual fear and the danger of violent death present it is probable that men cannot enjoy the fruits of their labor (as men in a community), the benefits of agriculture, industry, navigation, arts, letters, and science. It is significant that he also "lists" no account of time as a demoralizing factor. As a creature with a past and a future man is in time; his memory, his traditions, his accomplishments, his history are all expressions of his life in time. Where there is no account of time man forgets who he is and is reduced from the life of a man to that of an inhuman animal. Accounting of time is a social virture which in giving continuity to the community supplants mere instinct by the lessons of the past so that man may have a present that is meaningful to him and a future for which he may plan.

Peace is a communal virtue which makes possible and, it is hoped, probable the accomplishment of the goods of society. Hobbes, rather than the individualist that some hold him to be, recognizes the truth of the Greek view of man as a political animal although he explores it in his own way. Politics may be a science and the commonwealth an artifact; but the science of politics has as its end peace and the commonwealth is a creation of men, as man is a creation of God. That creation aims at man's purpose which is to live in peace in a community in order to realize the goods that a community has to offer to himself and others.

Let us now examine the creation of that public person, the generation of the commonwealth.

Since the vision of men pursuing their private interests privately is a vision that ends in war and the frustration of those interests, Hobbes points to a new vision for human happiness. We have argued that unless power and liberty are properly balanced, human happiness is not possible. Hobbes notes that power may be original as well as instrumental. Natural or original power refers to the abilities that a man has as an individual to obtain some future apparent good. It is a reflection of what he is as a creature. This is an amplification of his other statement on power in which he emphasized the inner capacity of an individual to move. In interpreting him we emphasized this as the stability necessary if "external" movement is to achieve those goods the individual desires.

Through his natural abilities, however, he may add to his store of capabilities; that is, he may work with his fellowmen or with nature itself to increase his reservoir. Nature and God may also present him with fortune or luck which adds to his original power. Hobbes holds that men are capable of achieving their greatest instrumental power when they unite for some common purpose. He states: "The greatest of human powers is that which is compounded of the powers of most men, united by consent, in one person, natural, or civil, that has the use of all their powers depending on his will, such as is the power of a commonwealth . . ." (III, 74). It becomes obvious to a student of Hobbes[9] that he found it difficult to work out the details by which the powers of many individuals could be united through consent in the generation of a public person. In what manner does one transfer power, and if consent is the vehicle does it include a mutual relationship with the person (be he one individual or many) whose will expresses the movement of that public person, i.e., the sovereign? If we consider original power then it is not possible for one literally to give his power to another; that is, one cannot become another. When one acts with authority he acts as his own director of action; that is, he is responsible for his behavior. When Hobbes uses the term *right* to account for this, he is not so much contrasting and comparing claims and duties as he is stressing the liberty that one has to use his own (original or instrumental) power to preserve himself. ("Preserve" in the fullest sense—that is, that one continues to live and to live well as seen, for instance, in those social goods mentioned earlier.) The liberty that one has to use one's power is, of course, a reflexive notion; for one must be free of external impediments, for example, chains, in order to use his power, that is, make actual his internal potentiality, and thus move about in the world. His right then, practically, is the absence of hindrance when he wishes to act. In effect, if his right were absent then he would no longer be at liberty. Hobbes often uses the term "obliged" as synonymous with "bound"; without examining whether this use is without moral connotations (which I would deny) it can at least be said that if one is bound or obliged with regard to X, then one is not at liberty to use his power regarding X. (Note that although obliged the individual yet retains his power.) "Right" in this sense means "freedom from obligation."[10]

Since one cannot give his power to another, Hobbes argues that what he can do is refrain from using it. He discusses two ways of doing this. He may refrain by renouncing his right. Regarding another person this would in effect remove him who renounces his right as an impediment to or competitor with that other. It does not increase the power of the other, but only his liberty. Hobbes holds that "by *simply* renouncing . . . he cares not to whom the benefit thereof redoundeth." It seems obvious that laying aside of right could hardly be the basis for compounding powers. One may quit the field, no longer be concerned with the chase, and leave the victory or the spoils to another. A "public" renunciation of this sort would, it seems, generally be temporary; there may be cases in which one renounces his right forever, but they would be few or far between. (Not that such a renunciation might not be very important both to the person renouncing and to whomever the benefit fell. One who "renounces" the world to enter a monastery or nunnery might be considered as giving up his or her right to use his or her power to secure future "earthly" goods.) It is obvious that without some compensation a permanent renunciation might quickly lead to infirmity or death.

Another way in which one lays aside his right is by transferring it "where he intended the benefit thereof to some certain person, or persons." Again it seems to me that here Hobbes has hardly provided the basis for compounding powers and hence for the generation of a commonwealth. It is a moot point whether or not in transferring one's right he "permits" its use to be dependent upon the will of another.[11] To put it more clearly, one would not be obliged to obey another regarding the use of one's power merely by intending the benefit to that other. Furthermore, in seeking peace through the generation of the commonwealth, Hobbes would hardly have provided that stability which he thinks necessary to it through this kind of transferring of power.

In the two ways discussed, Hobbes, it seems to me, is struggling to preserve his view that power must come from those individuals who will make up the subjects or members of the commonwealth. Their failure to govern themselves in that condition which he describes as the states of nature and of war drives them, as we have mentioned, to seek another way out. But merely renouncing or transferring their right to use their power is not sufficient to establish a body politic with moral as well as physical sanctions regarding their actions within that body. Rather than a loose collection of individuals grudgingly relinquishing their right to everything and a weak sovereign incapable of governing during domestic and foreign crises, a commonwealth is needed in which civic virtue unites its subjects while justice and the public good motivate its sovereign.

The way in which Hobbes supplemented the transference of power was to insist that its use by the sovereign (be it a monarchy, a democratic assembly, or an oligarchy) be authorized. Through the concept of authorization or representation, power was not merely transferred but the public representative was given authority to use the power of his subjects for public purpose. In authorization Hobbes claims that consent or concord in the establishment of civil authority is transformed as it were into a real unity.

That real unity is found in the generation of a "new" body, the body politic. The political body as analogous to the human body that we noted earlier in Harvey's work on the motion of the heart and blood is taken over by Hobbes. His famous introduction to *Leviathan* states that not only does the art of man imitate nature in making artificial life by way of automata, but, "*art* goes yet further, imitating that rational and most excellent work of nature, *man*. For by art is created that great LEVIATHAN called a COMMONWEALTH, or STATE, in Latin CIVITAS, which is but an artificial man; though of greater stature and strength than the natural, for whose protection and defence it was intended . . ." (III, ix). Since men in and of themselves as natural bodies cannot govern themselves sufficiently to make and keep peace, and since as natural bodies they cannot transfer to one another their power, it becomes necessary for them to create or generate a new body that will include them as parts and will have the use of their power so that it may act in their interest to protect and defend them and to maintain peace. The use of their power must be authorized and in this very authorization they generate that body. The generation of *Leviathan* establishes in nature, as it were, a civil creature created to resemble man. Civil power (civil authority), civil law, civil liberty, etc., are brought into being. Since self-government failed, authorized, representative government is given the task of establishing peace and promoting the general welfare. Part II of *Leviathan* is a detailed and brilliant analysis of the meaning of these concepts within the body politic.

The transference of the right to use power by the individual, and the authorization of its use, is not done in terms of self-love and selfish interest. It involves self-sacrifice, self-restraint, and dedication to peace as well as a heightening sense of civil virtue. The passions which men follow *without* government or which lead to the dissolution of government are natural. As Hobbes points out regarding them: "The desires, and other passions of man, are in themselves no sin. No more are the actions, that proceed from those passions, till they know a law that forbids them: which till laws be made they cannot know: nor can any law be made, till they have agreed upon the person that shall make it" (III, 114). Although the passions and reason are natural to man, "justice and injustice are none of the faculties neither of the body, nor mind. If they were, they might be in a man that were alone in the world, as well as his senses, and passions. They are qualities that relate to men in society, not in solitude" (III, 115). The making of that public person and the establishment of justice and injustice within that person change man's nature from an amoral individual to a creature whose passionate actions will be judged by a standard. As part of a new person he comes under the law established by that person. The purpose of that law is the individual's good; the price he pays for that is curtailment of his natural desires. This is hardly conducive to self-love, but it is an instance of dedication and sacrifice.

At this point it would be profitable to bring into our discussion Hobbes's development of the laws of nature. For they provide, along with the transference of the right one has to use his power and the authorization of that use by a public person, the fundamental attitudes and ground rules which make peace possible and the health and vitality of that new person probable. In the give-and-take that occurs while men pursue goods privately, a give-and-take which Hobbes holds leads to war, men learn about those states of affairs which make life solitary, poor, nasty, brutish, and short. In generalizing upon their experience, they express themselves by means of precepts or rules that are guides to their conduct. Although they may be so considered, these are not stated merely as hypotheticals of the sort "if you wish to achieve such and such, then you ought to do this or that." Rather are they stated as laws or commands which *forbid* a man to do that which is destructive of his life, or to take away the means of preserving it, or to omit that by which he thinks it might best be preserved. Hobbes had called that state a state of nature and those precepts learned through the experience of surviving in that state he calls "laws of nature." The laws of nature are not merely guides to individual conduct in war, they are also guides to the sovereign in his conduct of domestic and, perhaps, foreign affairs. As we shall see, they are not concerned only with bare preservation in war but with the establishment of peace. In this sense Hobbes calls them "convenient articles of peace." Since they forbid and oblige one regarding his conduct they are not to be confused with the right of nature in which he is at liberty to act.

In discussing the move from acts performed by private individuals to the generation of a public person whose judgments will set the domain of public action as well as those acts to be performed within that domain, Hobbes turns to those general precepts or rules by which the individual will guide his actions (a guide to the transference of rights). Just as the right of nature stated the liberty that a man had to use his power to preserve himself as he saw fit, so following the law (laws) of nature will oblige him (or bind him) regarding that right. Since while the right of nature prevailed in the state of nature the latter was concomitant with the state of war, the first and second laws of nature aim at the changing of both the justification for and the direction of a man's acts. "Seek peace," which is the first law, does not so much enjoin one to perform a particular act designated as peace-producing as it enjoins one to change his attitude. To seek peace is not to seek war; it is possible that no man seeks war but if "this natural right of every man to everything endureth, there can be no security to any man. . . ." It is something like saying "change your ways" or "be born again." It prepares the way for one no longer to be his own judge in all matters. The second law picks up this theme and asserts it. One should be willing (have the proper attitude), when others are also willing, to lay down his right to all things and be contented with so much liberty against other men as he would allow them against himself. It is worth remembering that the first law of nature also restated the right of nature; where peace is not possible one may defend himself by any means. (All is fair in love and war—especially war.) The first two laws are much like meta-laws. Be prepared to oblige (bind) yourself in the cause of peace; do this first by seeking peace. By so conditioning themselves, a multitude prepare themselves for the laying down of their right to everything, an act of self-sacrifice, and for the authorization of the use of their power by another, an act of selflessness. Hobbes's third law of nature is the font of justice. Perform those covenants made. Seek peace, divest oneself of one's right to all things, keep agreements. These injunctions are similar to those that might appear in a preamble to a constitution.

Hobbes's list of the laws of nature and his explanation of them continue the transference of a person who relies only upon himself to one who is fit for a community. The remaining laws are all in the puritan and liberal tradition (what has come to be called that). They hardly set down Hobbes as an authoritarian but rather as one who provides the basis for a constitution in which the action of a people united for peace culminates in the ordination and establishment of a government (sovereignty). Let us review some of those laws (III, chap. XV).[12] The fourth, gratitude, calls for goodwill, benevolence, trust, and reconciliation— virtues conducive to peace. The fifth directs that every man strives to accommodate himself to the rest so that men be sociable toward one another. The sixth is pardon; that upon caution of future time, a man ought to pardon the offenses past of those who repent and desire forgiveness; again, pardon is a key to peace. His seventh law provides a model for those who argue that punishment ought essentially be rehabilitative: ". . . *in revenges,* that is, retribution of evil for evil, *men look not at the greatness of the evil past, but the greatness of the good to follow.* Whereby we are forbidden to inflict punishment with any other design, than for the correction of the offender . . . revenge without respect to example, and profit to come is a triumph or glorying in the hurt of another . . ." (III, 140). Hobbes points out that this amounts to hurt without reason, which tends toward war, is against the law of nature, and is what we call "cruelty." In the ninth law he restates the equality of men and much of his discussion rests upon the oft-stated (by Hobbes) view that equality is fundamental to peace. He argues: "For there are very few so foolish, that had not rather govern themselves, than be governed by others: nor when the wise in their own conceit, contend by force, with them who distrust their own wisdom, do they always, or often, or almost at any time, get the victory. If nature have made men equal; that equality is to be acknowledged: or if nature have made men unequal; yet because men that think themselves equal, will not enter into conditions of peace, but upon equal terms, such equality must be admitted" (III, 141).

Here then is (what became) a cornerstone of social contract theory. Whether men are equal in power or not (for it is equality in power with which we are concerned, be that power original or instrumental) if we are to have peace and establish government, then those from whom authority (power) must come have to enter into that agreement as equals. Otherwise the conditions that lead to war yet prevail; men looking upon themselves as individuals with unusual power capable of satisfying their needs regardless of others inevitably come into conflict. Liberty without equality is a condition for war. Equality is closely related to equity and in the eleventh law Hobbes holds that *"if a man be trusted to judge between man and man,* it is a precept of the law of nature, *that he deal equally between them"* (III, 142).

In chapter XXX of *Leviathan*, Hobbes further discusses equity in terms of the administration of justice by the sovereign. He states: "The safety of the people, requireth further, from him, or them that have the sovereign power, that justice be equally administered to all degrees of people; that is, that as well the rich and mighty, as poor and obscure persons, may be righted of the injuries done them; so as the great, may have no greater hope of impunity, when they do violence, dishonour, or any injury to the meaner sort, than when one of these, does the like to one of them: for in this consisteth equity; to which, as being a precept of the law of nature, a sovereign is as much subject, as any of the meanest of his people" (III, 332). Hobbes clearly indicates not only that the sovereign is subject to the law of nature, but also that his violation of it will result in the ruin of the common-wealth. But I shall return to this shortly.

Without further examination of the laws of nature or the fact that Hobbes sees all of them summed up in the Golden Rule (III, 144), it may be said that as precepts they express the wisdom needed for peace-making. It is also obvious that they are ad-dressed as much or more to the sovereign as they are to individu-als. This indicates that Hobbes's state of nature is not to be taken as a precondition for the state or even society. One could hardly have learned all that is conducive to peace as indicated in the laws of nature had there not been civil society. Hobbes's task is to make peace and it is to its conditions that he puts much, if not all, of his genius to work. The state of war occurs when civil society cannot endure in peace. The laws of nature appear to me to be the precursor to the modern development of a constitution. Although at times Hobbes claims that the authority of the sover-eign is or ought to be without stint, he also claims that he is bound by the laws of nature. It is important to remember that the sovereign refers to the commonwealth or public person gen-erated and not merely to its representative as king, parliament, or aristocratic assembly. Hobbes also holds that in all sovereign-ties the laws of nature ought to be made civil law by the sover-eign. But these laws as noted direct the public person in their enactment so that peace, equity, liberty of subjects, and justice may prevail. In this sense the laws resemble a bill of rights limit-ing government in its governing of its people. It is in the laws of nature that the substance of the social contract is found in Hobbes; it is in the laws of nature that the moral responsibilities of government are found. The judgment upon the sovereign is in terms of both right and consequence. God will judge the rectitude of his laws and actions; a candid world and his subjects will judge the consequences of them.

The laws of nature, then, not only aim at obliging or binding one in his right to act unhindered (without justice), but they also redirect one's action toward the structure and continuity of a community. By putting oneself under law not only is one prevented from doing as he will, but one also places oneself under the commands of the lawgiver or legislator. Let us review the manner in which this is accomplished.

Hobbes does not support the view that God is the author of sovereignty; there is not a divine right of kings to exercise authority over subjects. Instead, he looks to men created in the image of the Creator to create through art a public person. Since they cannot literally give that public person power as they were given power, they must unite their own power instrumentally and then place it under the authority of the sovereign so that it becomes the original power of a public person. As noted earlier, the power to act, one's capability of acting, depends upon one's physical and mental being. One's liberty depends upon the absence of external impediments. One's power was also seen as most effective when one was "internally" stable. The laws of nature provide the basis for stability within the commonwealth. Authorizing the representative, as sovereign, to direct public power creates both the power of the government and the obligation of the people to obey. For by transferring their right to use their power and by authorizing the sovereign to command them in the use of that power, they both strip themselves of their liberty to act as their own sovereign with their own judgment (all this as a collection of individuals not united) and delegate the use of their power united to a representative, be he one or many. In this way they establish their obligation to obey the authorized commands of the sovereign.

It is in this sense that a commonwealth is established; authorized use of power is a condition of stability. This is the proper sense of "establishment" to make stability present within the nation. The public person in order to use his power (authority) in acting, both domestically and in foreign affairs, must be stable. The people united who make up the public person (recall the illustration on the frontispiece of the first edition of *Leviathan* showing the monarch as sovereign representative made up of his subjects) cannot pursue their own ends in liberty without a stable, authorized public person within which the goods of the community take form and become objects of a felicitous life. Hobbes notes in the generation of a commonwealth the importance of both transference of right and authorization of command; to give that body politic both the power to act and the liberty to use that power. In defining commonwealth he says: *". . . it is one person, of whose acts a great multitude, by mutual covenants one with another, have made themselves everyone the author, to the end he may use the strength and means of them all, as he shall think expedient, for their peace and common defence"*(III, 158). He had stated that in so doing the people had accomplished more "than consent or concord; it is a real unity of them all, in one and the same person . . ." (III, 158). Note carefully that this use of power and authority has nothing to do with force or violence. Power and authority are conditions for moral conduct on the part of government and subjects; force or violence indicate either the subjection of the lawless or the unauthorized use of power.

The public person is born out of the knowledge learned from experience, the capacity to formulate dictates of reason based upon that experience, and the ability to generate bodies given to men created in God's image. That public body is not an object of faith as God is but of reason and experience. Objects both of faith and of reason and experience may have the same end for mankind—peace; as such they are objects of reverence, respect, and awe. The sovereign God has the welfare of his creatures at heart, and their salvation is a condition of their living according to his dictates and the gift of his grace. Their submission to him, however, is an act of their will. Consent binds men to God and sovereign. Consent includes transference of right and authorization of power, both within the context of the laws of nature.

That mortal God, *Leviathan*, is also dedicated to their welfare and peace so that they may prepare the way for the coming of God to rule on earth. It is beyond the scope of this paper to enter into this aspect of Hobbes's philosophy, but a kingdom at peace is the precondition for the return of that peaceable kingdom and the reign of Christ on earth. He argues for this in part III of

Leviathan, especially chapter XXXVIII. The responsibility for a kingdom at peace as we have shown rests both with sovereign and with subjects. The latter are obliged to obey him in terms of the generation of that commonwealth—their consent to transfer their right of nature and authorize his use of their united power. They bind themselves so that they no longer are at liberty to use their power, and they authorize him to use it so that he may be a mortal god—powerful enough to handle public problems. In giving the sovereign that right they have no right against him and he cannot injure them. In using his power, however, he must abide by the laws of nature lest he bring about his ruin and that of his subjects. Liberty and power properly united are conducive to peace. Liberty without authority leads to anarchy and war. Authority without liberty leads to tyranny and war. If the sovereign returns the people to a state of war, the public person whom he represents may well become a casualty of that war.

Hobbes, we have argued, tried to point out the conditions that would lead to peace. Peace within the body politic rests upon transference of right and authorization of the use of power. That is why Hobbes stresses authority and its establishment. There can be no peace without it. Properly established it provides the internal order which makes action possible, action dedicated to the end of government and the needs, desires, and hopes of its subjects. No body can endure or preserve itself without internal stability. To be at liberty to use power, when that power is uncontrollable, is to have liberty without direction. "Anarchy of the body" is useless power. When power is properly united (powers within a private or public body) then it can be used efficiently for the good of that body. By generating a commonwealth within which the liberty and power of sovereign and subjects are properly ordered, men make possible the security of goods and a peaceful, contented life thereby. Hobbes saw this accomplished through transference of right, authorization of power, and implementation of the laws of nature. He made good use of Harvey's model of a human body with power and health through internal stability and wise behavior. Hobbes's discussion of the nutrition and procreation of a commonwealth (III, chap. XXIV) is a marvelous application of Harvey's description.[13] By his artful creation of Leviathan Hobbes hoped to pass between the points of liberty and authority unwounded.

THE PIETY OF HOBBES
by Herbert W. Schneider

THE HISTORY of mankind's philosophic cries for peace from ancient times to the present must include an imposing literature
of enlightened religion and desperate faith. To be genuinely philosophical such cries must combine a respect for peace of mind
with a hope for peace on earth. They must be more than apoca-
lyptic prophecies of a future bliss and less than illusory theories
of collective security. It is in this context that I call attention to
the faith and piety of Hobbes. His eloquent, passionate, and
rational confession in a time of violence, revolution, and experi-
ment gives to his philosophy an enduring vitality and relevance.
A decent historical setting for understanding Hobbes would require, in addition to a general acquaintance with the turmoil of
his time, a study of such contemporaries as Milton, Spinoza,
Malebranche, and Pascal. In this sketch I must take this setting
for granted, because this portrait of his religious feelings and
ideas is intended less as an example of philosophical piety among
his contemporaries, more as a work of pioneering for the Enlightenment that followed.

The central observation that seemed clear and distinct to
Hobbes is: man naturally needs peace and naturally makes war;
therefore man must discover a way to make peace. Since man

seems evidently incapable of being self-governing, he finds it necessary to authorize government and submit to it. A government, though duly authorized, cannot maintain itself in power unless it is enlightened by the science of natural justice and observes the universal prescriptions for peace. Similarly, citizens must learn that a commonwealth is dependent on such enlightenment. It is possible to get a clear statement of this faith as a moral and political theory in the secular parts of Hobbes's writings. But the fact remains that none of his writings are merely secular. We get a wrong impression of the man if we overlook, as is now commonly done, his personal piety and religious beliefs. The theory of personal salvation was an essential part of his philosophy and a major issue in the bitter conflicts of his time. To imagine that Hobbes was not personally concerned with these issues is sheer caricature and on the face of it highly improbable. Even in the first version of his theory of commonwealth, *De Cive*, a large portion (now usually omitted) is devoted to his justification, by biblical texts, of his unpopular religious stand on a central issue. He was surrounded by friends who believed that it would be a sin to obey the commands of their earthly sovereign, which seemed to them contrary to the commands of the divine sovereign. Hobbes's willingness to be law-abiding in such circumstances was not easy to justify either to his friends or to himself. He found it necessary to make a radical examination of the grounds of his own piety and of his theocratic covenant. What follows is his own summary of the arguments and conclusions. It is important to have this confession in Hobbes's own clear, passionate language. But it may be useful to make a few preliminary remarks on his rhetorical and symbolical use of the terms *Leviathan* and *Behemoth*, (as titles for his two major English works; they serve to give a religious tone to the subject matter.

Reference to these two beasts is incidental to the poetry of Job and to the appeals of some of the Prophets. References to them among Christian writers were less frequent than among the Talmudic authors, but not insignificant. In secular Hebrew "leviathan" means "whale" and "behemoth" means "hippopotamus," but as proper names in the mythology Leviathan (crocodile, curled snake, or dragon) is consistently the symbol of the powers of evil, more explicitly so than Behemoth, which is a monstrous, rather than an evil, beast. Both beasts were to be ultimately destroyed and sacrificed at the "messianic feast" when God finally would assert his absolute power over all others. But Hobbes makes Leviathan a symbol for a power that is to be dreaded reverently as an animal symbol for an almighty being; whereas Behemoth is the root of all evil. Hobbes, in his review (after the Restoration) of the British civil wars and of the villains and vices that caused them, entitles the work *Behemoth*. His exposition of "commonwealth" and more specifically of "Christian commonwealth," published in 1651 under Cromwell, is entitled *Leviathan* and contains this famous passage: "The multitude so united in one person is called a Common-wealth, in Latin *Civitas*. This is the generation of that great Leviathan, or rather (to speak more reverently) of that Mortal God, to which we owe under the Immortal God, our peace and defence" (chap. XVII). Hobbes does not explain his reverence for Leviathan's power, but the references in the traditional literature that may have been in his mind are two verses in Job, which (within the description of a dragonlike beast) refer to the Leviathan as a power with whom one cannot make a covenant (41:4) and as "king over all the sons of pride" (41:34). This was apparently useful rhetoric for Hobbes.

The central themes of the passages that will be cited state the problem of how the following aspects of law and morality are related to each other: (1) the commands of an earthly sovereign; (2) the law of the land which the king's courts would use to justify the commands as laws; (3) the "natural law" of the kingdom of God by nature which is equivalent to the universal principles of peace and of rational prudence; (4) the Mosaic Commandments which God used to govern his chosen people, Israel; and (5) the "spiritual laws" of the Heavenly Kingdom of Christ. In distinguishing these types of government Hobbes is also distinguishing between justice and piety, between "true religion" and ecclesiastical superstructures, between obedience to the Spiritual Sovereign, Christ, and obedience to earthly sovereigns. The practical conclusion is that it is not sin to obey a temporal sovereign (unless he commands repudiation of "true religion" or belief in salvation through Christ), nor is it a sin to disobey popes, bishops, or Presbyterian ministers if they claim to have independent authority from God direct to command obedience (whether in "spiritual" or "temporal" affairs) in opposition to the jurisdiction of a secular government that has legitimacy or "divine right." Evidently, the central issue is, What is divine right? On this issue Hobbes had a new, intricate theory of "representation," which involved him in no less a problem than the nature of the three "persons" in the Divine Trinity.

I cite first from *De Cive,* then from *Leviathan,* and lastly from *Behemoth* in order to show that Hobbes repeats the essentials in all three, when he was personally under very different political circumstances.

De Cive

Were the nature of human actions as distinctly known as the nature of quantity in geometrical figures, the strength of avarice and ambition, which is sustained by the erroneous opinions of the vulgar, as touching the nature of right and wrong, would presently faint and languish, and mankind should enjoy such an immortal peace, that (unless it were for habitation, on supposition that the earth should grow too narrow for her inhabitants) there would hardly be left any pretence for war. . . . There is a certain clue of reason, whose beginning is in the dark, but by the benefit of whose conduct, we are led as it were by the hand into the clearest light, so that the principle of tractation is to be taken from that darkness, and then the light to be carried thither for irradiating its doubts. . . . When I applied my thoughts to the investigation of natural justice . . . I found that this proceeded not from nature, but consent. . . . I have demonstrated by a most evident connection . . . first the absolute necessity of leagues and contracts, and thence the rudiments both of moral and civil prudence. That appendage which is added concerning the regiment of God, hath been done with this intent, that the dictates of God Almighty in the law of nature, might not seem repugnant to the written law, revealed to us in his word (*The Epistle Dedicatory*).

In this book thou shalt find briefly described the duties of men, first as men, then as subjects, lastly, as Christians; under which duties are contained not only the elements of the law of nature, and of nations, together with the true original and power of justice, but also the very essence of Christian religion itself (*Preface to the Reader*).

I show how the sovereign powers repugn not the divine right, for as much as God overrules all rulers by nature, that is, by the dictates of natural reason . . . God doth now rule over us Christians by virtue of our covenant of baptism; and therefore the authority of rulers in chief, or of civil government, is not at all, we see, contrary to religion. . . . These things I found most bitterly excepted against: that I had made the civil powers too large, but this by ecclesiastical persons; that I had utterly taken away liberty of conscience, but this by sectaries; that I had set princes above the civil laws, but this by lawyers. Wherefore I was not much moved by these men's reprehensions (*Preface to the Reader*).

There are three manners whereby we are said to hear God: right reasoning, sense, and faith. God's sensible word hath come but to few; neither hath God spoken to men by revelation except particularly to some, and to diverse diversely; neither have any laws of his kingdom been published in this manner unto any people. . . . Because the word of God, ruling by nature only, is supposed to be nothing else but right reason, and the laws of kings can be known by their word only, it is manifest that the laws of God, ruling by nature alone, are only the natural laws. . . . Reason dictates one name alone which doth signify the nature of God, that is, existent, or simply, that he is; and one in order to, and in relation to us, namely God, under which is contained both King, and Lord, and Father. . . . God must be worshipped not privately only, but openly and publicly in the sight of all men; because that worship is so much the more acceptable, by how much it begets honour and esteem in others. . . . We must use our best endeavour to keep the laws of nature. For the undervaluing of our master's command, exceeds all other affronts whatsoever; as on the other side, obedience is more acceptable than all other sacrifices. . . . If subjects worship not God . . . if they confess not before men, both in words and deeds, that there is one God, most great, most good, most blessed, the Supreme King of the world and of all worldly kings, this is the sin of treason against the Divine Majesty. For it is a denying of the Divine Power, or atheism. . . .

When we say, I believe in Christ, we signify indeed whom we believe, but not what we believe. Now, to believe in Christ is nothing else but to believe that Jesus is the Christ, namely he, who according to the prophecies of Moses and the prophets of Israel, was to come into this world to institute the kingdom of God. . . . To a Christian there is no other article of faith requisite as necessary to salvation, but only this, that Jesus is the Christ. . . . If any man be displeased that I do not judge all those eternally damned, who do not inwardly assent to every article defined by the Church (and yet do not contradict, but, if they be commanded, do submit), I know not what I shall say to them. For the most evident testimonies of Holy Writ, which do follow, do withhold me from altering my opinion (chap. XV).

That the same obedience, even from a Christian subject, is due in all temporal matters to those princes who are no Christians, is without any controversy; but in matters spiritual, that is to say, those things which concern God's worship, some Christian Church is to be followed. . . . But what? Must we resist princes when we cannot obey them? Truly, no; for this is contrary to our civil covenant. What must we do then? Go to Christ by martyrdom; which if it seem to any man to be a hard saying, most certain it is that he believes not with his whole heart, that Jesus is the Christ, the Son of the living God (chap. XVIII).

Leviathan

Our Saviour, both in teaching and reigning, representeth (as Moses did) the Person of God, which God from that time forward, but not before, is called the "Father," and being still one and the same substance, is one person as represented by Moses and another person as represented by his Son the Christ. For "Person" being a relative to a representer, it is consequent to plurality of representers that there be a plurality of persons, though of one and the same substance. . . .

Seeing then our Saviour hath denied his kingdom to be in this world, seeing he hath said he came not to judge but to save the world, he hath not subjected us to other laws than those of the commonwealth; that is, the Jews to the Law of Moses (which he saith he came not to destroy but to fulfil) and other nations to the laws of their several sovereigns, and all men to the Laws of

Nature, the observing whereof both he himself and his Apostles
have in their teaching recommended to us, as a necessary condition of being admitted by him in the last day into his eternal
kingdom, wherein shall be protection and life everlasting. Seeing
then our Saviour and his Apostles left not new laws to oblige us
in this world, but new doctrine to prepare us for the next, the
books of the New Testament which contain that doctrine, until
obedience to them was commanded by them that God had given
power to on earth to be legislators, were not obligatory canons,
that is, laws, but only good and safe advice for the direction of
sinners in the way to salvation, which every man might take and
refuse at his own peril without injustice. . . .

Spiritual commonwealth there is none in this world, for it is
the same thing with the Kingdom of Christ, which he himself
saith is not of this world, but shall be in the next world, at the
Resurrection, when they that have lived justly and believed that
he was the Christ shall, though they died *natural* bodies, rise
spiritual bodies; and then it is, that our Saviour shall judge the
world, and conquer his adversaries and make a spiritual commonwealth. In the meantime, seeing that there are no men on earth,
whose bodies are spiritual, there can be no spiritual commonwealth among men who are yet in the flesh (chap. XLI).

"Church" (when not taken for a house) signifieth the same that
"ecclesia" signified in the grecian commonwealths, that is to say,
a Congregation or an Assembly of citizens called forth to hear
the magistrate speak unto them. . . . The Church can be taken
for one person: that is to say, that it can be said to have power
to will, to pronounce, to command, to be obeyed, to make laws,
or to do any other action whatsoever. For without authority from
a lawful congregation, whatsoever act be done in a concourse of
people, it is the particular act of every one of those that were
present . . . There is on earth no such universal church as all
Christians are bound to obey, because there is no power on earth
to which all other commonwealths are subject. . . . "Temporal"
and "spiritual" government are but two words brought into the
world to make men see double and mistake their lawful sovereign
(chap. XXXIX).

A Sacrament is a separation of some visible thing from common use; and a consecration of it to God's service for a sign either
of our admission into the Kingdom of God to be of the number
of His peculiar people, or for a commemoration of the same . . .
As it implies an oath or promise of allegiance to God, there were
no other sacraments in the Old Testament but circumcision and

the Passover; nor are there any other in the New Testament but baptism and the Lord's Supper (chap. XXXVI).

The king and every other sovereign executeth his office of Supreme Pastor by immediate authority from God . . . From this consolidation of the right politic and ecclesiastic in Christian sovereigns it is evident they have all manner of power over their subjects that can be given to men for the government of men's external actions both in policy and religion, and may make such laws as themselves shall judge fittest for the government of their own subjects, both as they are the commonwealth and as they are the church, for both state and church are the same men. If they please, therefore, they may (as many Christian kings now do) commit the government of their subjects in matters of religion to the Pope, but then the Pope is in that point subordinate to them and exerciseth that charge in another's dominion *jure civili*, in the right of the civil sovereign, not *jure divino*, in God's right, and may therefore be discharged of that office, when the sovereign for the good of his subjects shall think it necessary. They may also if they please commit the care of religion to one supreme pastor or to an assembly of pastors and give them what power over the church or one over another they think most convenient. . . .

All governments which men are bound to obey are simple and absolute. . . . And of the three sorts of government which is the best is not to be disputed where any one of them is already established, but the present ought always to be preferred, maintained, and accounted best, because it is against both the law of nature and the divine positive law to do anything tending to the subversion thereof (chap. XLII).

It is not the Roman clergy only that pretends the Kingdom of God to be of this world, and thereby to have a power therein, distinct from that of the civil state. And this is all I had a design to say concerning the doctrine of the politics, which when I have reviewed, I shall willingly expose it to the censure of my country (chap. XLVII).

Behemoth

It is a hard matter for men, who do all think highly of their own wits, when they have also acquired the learning of the university,

NOTE: Page references for *Behemoth* are to the new and revised version of the Tönnies edition, 1969.

to be persuaded that they want any ability requisite for the government of a commonwealth, especially having read the glorious histories and the sententious politics of the ancient popular governments of the Greeks and Romans. . . . The Presbyterian ministers, in the beginning of the reign of Queen Elizabeth did not (because they durst not) publicly and plainly preach against the discipline of the Church. But not long after, by the favour perhaps of some great courtier, they went abroad preaching in most of the market-towns of England, as the preaching friars had formerly done, upon working-days in the morning; in which sermons, these and others of the same tenets, that had charge of souls, both by the manner and matter of their preaching, applied themselves wholly to the winning of the people to a liking of their doctrines and good opinion of their persons. . . .

Before their sermons, their prayer was or seemed to be *extempore*, which they pretended to be dictated by the spirit of God within them, and many of the people believed or seemed to believe it. For any man might see, that had judgment, that they did not take care beforehand what they should say in their prayers. And from hence came a dislike of the *common-prayer-book* which is a set form, premeditated, that men might see to what they were to say *Amen*. . . . They did never in their sermons, or but lightly, inveigh against the lucrative vices of men of trade or handicraft; such as are feigning, lying, cozening, hypocrisy, or other uncharitableness, except want of charity to their pastors and to the faithful: which was a great ease to the generality of citizens and the inhabitants of market-towns, and no little profit to themselves (pp. 23–25).

The mischief proceeded wholly from the Presbyterian preachers, who, by a long practised histrionic faculty, preached up the rebellion powerfully (p. 159).

The sting of Presbytery consisted in a severe imposing of odd opinions upon the people, impertinent to religion, but conducing to the advancement of the power of the Presbyterian ministers (p. 169).

It is impossible that the multitude should ever learn their duty, but from the pulpit and upon holidays; but then, and from thence, it is, that they learned their disobedience. And, therefore, the light of that doctrine has been hitherto covered and kept under here by a cloud of adversaries, which no private man's reputation can break through, without the authority of the *Uni-*

versities. But out of the *Universities* came all those preachers that taught the contrary. The *Universities* have been to this nation, as the wooden horse was to the Trojans (pp. 39–40).

What have we then gotten by our deliverance from the Pope's tyranny, if these petty men succeed in the place of it, that have nothing in them that can be beneficial to the public, except their silence? For their learning, it amounts to no more than an imperfect knowledge of Greek and Latin, and an acquired readiness in the Scripture language, with a gesture and tone suitable thereunto; but of justice and charity, the manners of religion, they have neither knowledge nor practice (p. 172).

I think they never would have ventured into the field, but for that unlucky business of imposing upon the Scots, who were all Presbyterians, our book of Common-prayer. . . . This gave occasion to the greatest part of the nobility and others to enter, by their own authority, into a Covenant amongst themselves, which impudently they called a *Covenant with God,* to put down episcopacy (p. 28).

Because the clergy in the Universities, by whom all things there are governed, and the clergy without the Universities, as well bishops as inferior clerks, did think that the pulling down of the Pope was the setting up of them (as to England) in his place, and made no question, the greatest part of them, but that their spiritual power did depend not upon the authority of the King, but of Christ himself, derived to them by a successive imposition of hands from bishop to bishop. . . . Though they were content that the divine right, which the Pope pretended to in England, should be denied him, yet they thought it not so fit to be taken from the Church of England, whom they now supposed themselves to represent. . . . For religion has been for a long time, and is now by most people, taken for the same thing with divinity, to the great advantage of the clergy. . . . To believe in Christ is nothing with them, unless you believe as they bid you. Charity is nothing with them, unless it be charity and liberality to them, and partaking with them in faction. How we can have peace while this is our religion, I cannot tell. . . . Religion should be a quiet waiting for the coming again of our blessed Saviour, and in the meantime a resolution to obey the King's laws (which also are God's laws); to injure no man, to be in charity with all men, to cherish the poor and sick, and to live soberly and free from scandal; without mingling our religion with points of natural philosophy, as freedom of will, incorporeal substance, everlasting nows, ubiquities, hypostases, which the people understand not, nor will ever care for (pp. 56–58).

I like not the design of drawing religion into an art, whereas it ought to be a law; and though not the same in all countries, yet in every country indisputable (p. 43).

I cannot think that preaching to the people the points of their duty, both to God and man, can be too frequent; so it be done by grave, discreet, and ancient men, that are reverenced by the people; and not by the light quibbling young men, whom no congregation is so simple as to look to be taught by (as being a thing contrary to nature), or to pay them any reverence, or to care what they say, except some few that may be delighted with their jingling. I wish with all my heart, there were enough such discreet and ancient men, as might suffice for all the parishes of England, and that they would undertake it. But this is but a wish (p. 64).

There are so many places of Scripture easy to be understood, that teach both true faith and good morality (and that as fully as is necessary to salvation), of which no seducer is able to dispossess the mind (of any ordinary readers), that the reading of them is so profitable as not to be forbidden without great danger to them and the commonwealth. . . . Neither children, nor the greatest part of men, do understand why it is their duty to do so. They see not that the safety of the commonwealth, and consequently of their own, depends upon their doing it. . . . Such men as have studied the Greek or Latin, or both tongues, and that are withal such as love knowledge, and consequently take delight in finding out the meaning of the most hard texts, or in thinking they have found it, in case it be new and not found out by others, these are therefore they, that praetermitting the easy places which teach them their duty, fall to scanning only of the mysteries of religion. Such as are: how it may be made out with wit, *That there be three that bear rule in heaven, and these three but one? How the Deity could be made flesh? How that flesh could be really present in many places at once? Where is the place, and what the torments, of hell?* And other metaphysical doctrines: *Whether the will of man be free, or governed by the will of God? Whether sanctity comes by inspiration or education?* . . . These and the like points are the study of the curious, and the cause of all our late mischief, and the cause that makes the plainer sort of men, whom the Scripture had taught belief in Christ, love towards God, obedience to the King, and sobriety of behaviour, forget it all, and place their religion in the disputable doctrines of these your wise men. . . . Whatsoever is necessary for them to know, is so easy, as not to need interpretation; whatsoever is more, does them no good (pp. 53–55).

This may suffice as an exposition of Hobbes's feelings and views on "true religion" and on the relations between scriptural, political, and scientific authority. His efforts to explore each of these types of authority thoroughly in order to clarify their relations made his philosophy impressive, complex, and unpopular. The complicated adjustments and judgments were practically forced on him by the revolutions of his time and country; he fled but did not evade the issues.

The narrative of *Behemoth* is excellent evidence of the struggles both in his environment and in himself. A few items in addition to the above may serve to throw further light on his personality and opinions. He thought that the civil wars might have been avoided if King Charles (who was less Scottish than James) had not forced the prayer book on the Scots. He emphasized this imposition despite his scorn for the Presbyterians and his love for the Book of Common Prayer. Hobbes also observed several times that the English and Scottish "nations" should not have regarded each other as "foreigners"; they were really a single "people." He (as did Bacon also) took for granted that the House of Stuart would promote a genuine fraternity. He also applauded Cromwell for bringing Scottish and Irish representatives into Parliament as soon as he came into control of the Rump.

In general, Cromwell emerges from the narrative as a hero and Charles I as a stubborn but conscientious martyr to sovereignty. He admitted that Charles was "right" but admired Cromwell for his ability to create the commonwealth by a series of strategies. The final sentence of *Behemoth* (after wishing King Charles II a long reign) is: "May the King have as often as there shall be need such a general [as Cromwell]. . . . I think the bringing of his little army entire out of Scotland to London, was the greatest stratagem that is extant in history."

Hobbes introduced the Restoration into his narrative in a significant way. He rejoiced that "the law" forced the Rump to call for new elections: "That brought in the King: for few of the Long

Parliament . . . could get themselves chosen again." To Hobbes
this event meant that in the future the sovereigns would rule "by
the Grace of God and the Will of the People," which became
their official title in 1689. Hobbes regarded his political philosophy as the theoretical foundation for this reconciliation of divine
right and representative government. Thus Hobbes prepared
some of the philosophical ground for Locke and the Glorious
Revolution. *Behemoth* was supposed to explain all this to Charles
II, who did not need to have it explained, and who regarded
Hobbes's history as inflammatory. He would not permit its publication.

The chief point, however, of this study of Hobbes as a person
is to describe his piety and "true religion." He was clearly an
orthodox Christian and, far from being an atheist, was devout.
He was a sincere Anglican without caring about episcopacy. He
was decidedly not a separatist, but like many of the Anglican
nonseparatist Puritans had Congregationalist sympathies. His
scorn for Presbyterian preachers and for High Church bishops
was extreme and outspoken; otherwise, his views on religion,
scholastic theology, morals, and science were shared by many of
his contemporaries.

His religious faith and piety may well be compared with that
of two prominent persons who were in many ways close to him:
Francis Bacon and John Milton. Milton, beginning at Cambridge
to hold religious views practically identical with those of Hobbes
at a Puritan college in Oxford, became an Independent (in
Hobbes's terms, a "sectarian") but came to embrace the views of
religious "illuminism," that is, of enlightenment by an indwelling Holy Spirit of perfect love. In his writings on Christian
doctrine he followed the Ramist model of making a basic distinction between "worship" and "doctrine" (as did Hobbes) and
treating each in a separate part of his treatise. But in his late little
tract on *True Religion* he is also explicit in basing worship on
supernatural enlightenment by an indwelling Holy Spirit. He
also makes a reference to this in *Samson Agonistes*.[1] He entertained,

too, some of the Unitarian doctrines. Though the early diatribes of their college days by both men were practically identical against scholastic philosophy and theology, Hobbes refused to embrace any of the "supernaturalist conversations" of the "enthusiasts" and confined his conception of enlightenment to "the light of nature," or reason. He remained an Anglican, taking communion in the church, though he refused to be seen in public with bishops, whom he regarded as subversives.

Hobbes was closer to Bacon religiously as well as philosophically. Bacon was more under Puritan influence than Hobbes, having been raised a Puritan by his mother. But their attitudes toward Oxford's scholasticism were the same; their early essays on the subject were very similar and show some traces of Ramist influence. As Bacon's secretary for a time (and apparently a favorite secretary) he probably shared some of Bacon's interests. Historians have discounted Bacon's influence on Hobbes, on the grounds that Hobbes was at that time preoccupied with classical studies, but it is quite possible that the closer investigations that are now being made of both Bacon and Hobbes will bring to light philosophical as well as literary sharing. In any case, the views of Hobbes on religious matters are so similar to Bacon's that I submit as relevant to Hobbes two religious compositions of Bacon. Bacon composed a creed and a prayer for his private use; they were not published until two decades after his death, when they appeared among "Bacon's Remaines" in 1648. However, both the creed and the prayer had been shown to members of Parliament in 1641 (then dominantly Puritan) as noteworthy expressions of "the orthodox reformed faith." "Reformed" in this context meant much more than "Anglican." A few excerpts will give the reader an idea of their general nature.

From Bacon's "Confession of the Truth"

I believe that nothing is without beginning but God, not nature, no matter, no spirit, but one only and the same God.

There are three times (if times they may be called) or parts of Eternity:

The first, The time before beginning, when the God-head was only without the being of any Creature.

The second, The time of Mystery, which continueth from the Creation to the dissolution of the World.

The third, The time of the Revelation of the Sons of God, which time is the last, and is without change.

Whensoever God doth break the law of nature by miracles (which are ever new Creatures) he never cometh to that point or passe, but in regard of the worke of Redemption.

The lawes of Nature, which now remaine and govern Inviolably till the end of the world, begin to be in force when God first rested from his works, and ceased to create. But received a revocation (in part) by the curse, since which time they changed not.

As at the first the Soule of Man was not produced by Heaven or earth but was breathed immediately from God: So that the wayes and proceedings from God with Spirits are not concluded in Nature, that is in the lawes of Heaven and Earth, but are reserved to the law of his secret will, and grace wherein God worketh still and resteth not from the work of Creation.

Then follows the Great Mystery and Perfect Centry of all God's ways, the Mediation of the Eternal Son of God.

After the coming of the Holy Ghost, the Teacher of all Truth, the booke of the Scriptures is shut . . . and the Church hath no power over the Scriptures to teach or command anything contrary to the written word.

There is also a Holy succession of the Prophets of the New Testament and Fathers of the Church from the time of the Apostles and Disciples which saw our Saviour in the flesh unto the consummation of the work of the Ministry, which persons are called of God, by guift or inward annointing and the vocation of God, followed by an outward calling or ordination of the Church.

From Bacon's "Prayer Made and Used by the Late Lord Chancellor"

O Eternal God, and most mercifull Father in Jesus Christ; in whom Thou hast made a Covenant of grace and mercy with all those that come unto Thee in him, in his name and mediation we humbly prostrate our selves before the throne of thy mercies seat acknowledging that by the breach of all thy holy lawes and commandments we are become wild olive branches, strangers to thy covenant of grace, we have defaced in our selves thy sacred Image imprinted in us by Creation. . . . O stay not the course of thy mercies and loving kindnesses towards us; Have mercy upon us O Lord for thy dear Sonne Christ Jesus sake, who is the way, the truth, and the life. . . . Turn our hearts, and we shall be turned, convert us and we shall be converted; illuminate the eyes of our mindes and understanding with the bright beames of the Holy Spirit, that we may dayly grow in the saving knowledge of the heavenly mystery of our redemption, wrought by our dear Lord and Saviour Jesus Christ. Sanctify our wils and affection by the same Spirit. . . . Inflame our hearts with thy love, cast forth of them what displeaseth thee, all infidelity, hardness of heart, prophanenesse, hypocrisie, contempt of thy holy word and ordinances, all uncleannesse. . . . Plant thy holy feare in our hearts . . . increase our weak faith . . . that by the power of his resurrection we may be quickened, and raised up to newnesse of life, may be truly born anew, and may be effectually made partakers of the first resurrection, that then the second death may never have dominion over us . . . that in the said divorce of soul and body we may be translated here to that Kingdom of Glory prepared for all those that love thee . . . Amen.

There is nothing in Hobbes's faith and piety that would lead us to think that he would not give to all this his "Amen." In the essentials of their faith and worship Milton, Bacon, and Hobbes were agreed. And they represent the enlightenment of their time. To dismiss all this as incompatible with their philosophies, or as mere protective coloration or social security, seems preposterous and betrays an inability to place these men in their time and circumstances. It should not take much historical knowledge to realize how different our perspective and world of imagination, to say nothing of religion, are from those of the seventeenth century. It is difficult, however, to appreciate the enormous changes in historical knowledge and criticism which separate these men not merely from a twentieth-century perspective but even from the Enlightenment of the late eighteenth century and the nineteenth century. The range of skepticism has grown to such an extent that it is almost impossible to realize that such faith and piety were common among men who even in their day were called atheists and skeptics.

Hobbes's philosophy came to life again early in the nineteenth century. Jeremy Bentham had prepared the way. For despite Bentham's dismissal of natural law and Christian piety, he and Hobbes had much in common: rational jurisprudence, anti–common law, commonwealth. It was therefore a genuine insight that led John Austin and his "analytic jurisprudence" to reconcile Bentham and Hobbes as heralds of what J. S. Mill called "radicalism." Hobbes himself might have been pleased to find himself as a champion of "the omnicompetence of the House of Commons" provided, of course, that there was no "His Majesty's Loyal Opposition." For he took a bourgeois pride in "the people of London" and in "the Scots" because they were accustomed, as he put it, to enjoy having kings reign not "over them" but "under them" (cf. *Behemoth*, p. 149). Hobbes even seemed to praise the reign of God Almighty for similar reasons. But in the nineteenth-century revival Hobbes was completely secularized and then even made a materialist, Epicurean atomist, mechanist, in addition to being an atheist. And this nineteenth-century disincarnation of Hobbes still lingers in the expositions of Hobbism minus Hobbes. A more radical enlightenment and impiety have produced a very different type of skeptic. As late as Bayle (also an enlightened Protestant!) we find him in his article on Hobbes in the *Dictionary* writing, "Il fit avouer aux plus clairvoyants, qu'on n'avait jamais si bien pénétré les fondaments de la politique."

Hobbes hoped that his tombstone would indicate that he was the discoverer of "the science of natural justice," but he would have been horrified to see his theory robbed of its natural piety and his person robbed of his Christian piety.

The *Leviathan* was a passionate sermon to a warring world, submitted first to Cromwell and then to his fellow citizens of the commonwealth. In it he made explicit the virtues that compose justice and secure peace; he formulated them so uncompromisingly and severely that he had little confidence that men would actually end their insecurity, both individual and collective, both civil and international, either by conscientious discipline or by just government. He conceived the task of making peace by justice and jurisprudence in all its practical difficulty. But beneath the sermon lay the philosopher's patient hope in the eventual coming on earth of the Kingdom of Christ, when peace and security will be enthroned by "natural justice." Here the adjective "natural" is eloquent, for it embodies Hobbes's faith that human reason and jurisprudence can adapt themselves eventually to the natural demands of the Almighty.

HOBBES'S ANGLICAN
DOCTRINE OF SALVATION

by Paul J. Johnson

HOBBES HAS BEEN the subject of controversy almost from the moment he set pen to paper and first involved himself in the burning political and religious issues which were to keep England in turmoil for a century. In the minds of many of his countrymen his willingness to expose the darker side of men's nature, his often unique interpretations of Scripture, his materialism, and his unrelenting Erastianism combined to make him seem an arch-villain. If some, like Harrington, appreciated his powers, others would willingly have burned him as an atheist. He was the sort of thinker who was both too brilliant to ignore and too caustic for many to embrace.

Hobbes, quite naturally, defended himself vigorously against such a dangerous charge as atheism and claimed always to be a good, obedient Christian. Few of his contemporaries seem to have been convinced by these protestations and yet today no substantial agreement has been reached concerning Hobbes's religion. The question lingers and infects our attempts to under-

NOTE: I wish to thank the librarian and the staff of the Huntington Library for the courtesy and assistance they extended me during my research for this paper and for permission to quote from their copies of rare books by Hobbes, Chillingworth, and Hales.

stand his political theory. Current opinion ranges from the belief that Hobbes's aim was nothing less than the total destruction of the religious view of life which, it is suggested, he detested to the opposite pole where he is identified as a Christian thinker whose political science is but a small part of a greater religious whole.[1] To all appearances commentators adopting positions on Hobbes's religious convictions have done so, with minor exceptions, without the benefit of more than a cursory glance at the historical climate in which Hobbes's doctrines were formed. The favored method of understanding Hobbes's claims seems to have been to contemplate the bare texts and await enlightenment. But few texts interpret themselves and this method suffers from a number of difficulties.[2] To mention but one example, the force of a remark cannot be assessed unless one is familiar with the linguistic conventions of the historical period in which it occurred. How is one to decide whether a remark is to be taken as a joke, a commonplace, a revolutionary insight, a formal obeisance, an insult, or a compliment without knowledge of the assumed truths, the commonplaces, the manners, and so on of its day?

Take for example the following remark by Hobbes: ". . . it is with the mysteries of our religion, as with wholesome pills for the sick; which swallowed whole have the power to cure; but chewed are mostly cast up again without effect."[3] Is it, with its epigrammatic compression and crude simile, the sarcasm of a disbeliever, or with its positive message of wholesome cures an assertion of the legitimacy of faith? Stephen and Flew cite it the one way, Robertson and Peters the other.[4] Clearly the remark itself contains characteristics to support either interpretation and no amount of meditating on it alone will tell us on which side of the skepticism-sincerity ledger this entry is to be recorded. Nor will comparison with Hobbes's other utterances on religion help since these are, for the most part, of equally Delphic force. Nor would the ability to integrate Hobbes's remarks on religion with the rest of his philosophy solve the problem, for then we would know only that his religious remarks maintained a formal coherence with his nonreligious ones. Their force, and hence their content, would remain opaque. To the extent that the religious remarks are connected with the nonreligious ones, the opaqueness will merely spread throughout the system rendering the whole more obscure.

What clarification is possible in such cases must come from an examination of the historical context in which the doubtful remarks occurred. Of course there is no guarantee that the intentions of an author can be recovered in this way. A careful, clever writer can always cover his tracks and a hypocritical one can adopt, out of convenience, positions he does not believe. But these possibilities should not prevent us from establishing what probabilities we can, any more than the possibility of unicorns should tempt us into ignoring the improbabilities of their existence. At least in this way the burden of proof is shifted to those who wish to assert the possibility in the face of the probabilities.

When Hobbes's remarks on the Christian mysteries, salvation, and religion are examined against the background of the religious developments of his own time, it can be clearly seen that his comparison of the mysteries to pills for the sick is not skeptical but is part and parcel of a doctrine of salvation and a theory of Christianity which formed the mainstream of Anglican doctrinal development in the seventeenth century. Furthermore this development received much of its impetus from the writings of men who almost certainly were among Hobbes's acquaintances and with whom he may have frequently associated. In the next section I will illustrate the main thrust of this movement from the writings of two such men and then in the succeeding section attempt to show that Hobbes's position is substantially indistinguishable from theirs.

As a preliminary to this it will be well to remove one possible sticking point. It might seem obvious to the modern ear that anyone who would compare the Christian mysteries to pills being chewed, swallowed, and vomited up could not be very serious about those mysteries. But sensibilities change and the seventeenth century was not so delicate about references to bodily functions in serious writing as we, until recently, have been.

Even when dealing with the most serious religious matters, the tendency was to make the point and let the allusions fall where they might.[5] William Laud, for example, could refer to grace as "spiritual eyewater," an image that would sound uncouth coming from a modern divine. Our own impressions of the tone of a remark, as well as our assessment of its force, must be corrected by familiarity with the conventions of its historical origins. Hobbes's image of mysteries chewed, swallowed, and cast up would have carried little emotive impact in his own day.

I

The problem facing Anglican thinkers in the seventeenth century was to discover a route by which a middle course might be sailed between the Scylla of Roman Catholicism and the Charybdis of the enthusiastic Protestantism of the Presbyterians and Independents. Their doctrinal strategy centered on two points: the categorical denial of infallibility and the drawing of a distinction between fundamentals and accessories of faith. The first point hit both antagonists. On the one side the papal claim of authority to establish new dogma was attacked, on the other the claim of individuals to authoritative inner enlightenment. Both claims were fertile sources of controversy. As Hooker put it, "Two things there are which trouble greatly these later times: one that the Church of Rome cannot, another that Geneva will not, err."[6]

As a counterpoise to these claims of interpretative infallibility, the Anglicans argued for a simplified Christianity whose essence lay in a very few fundamental doctrines which had been so clearly presented in the Scriptures as to require no interpretation and no special qualifications to understand beyond the simple willingness to read the words without prejudice. Salvation required belief in these doctrines alone; other beliefs, whatever they might be, were matters of indifference. Thus the infallibility of men and institutions was replaced in Anglican thought with the simpleness and clarity of fundamental doctrines.

Both positions were rooted at the onset of the century in

Hooker's *Laws of Ecclesiastical Polity* and were further developed in the early part of the century by such men as John Hales and William Chillingworth. The latter were members, along with Hobbes, of the brilliant circle of scholars and writers who gathered at Lord Falkland's home, Great Tews, some twelve miles outside Oxford where the library was said to rival that of the university. Besides Hobbes, Hales, and Chillingworth, the circle included Hobbes's friends Sidney Godolphin and George Eglionby, later dean of Canterbury, and the poets Jonson and Suckling as well as lesser lights, many of whose talents were, however, sufficient to earn them bishoprics in the Anglican Church.[7] It was in the library of Great Tews that Chillingworth spent the years 1628 to 1638 composing his massive *The Religion of Protestants a Safe Way to Salvation*, a work of some four hundred folio pages which became a foundation stone of Anglican thought.[8]

Chillingworth had come to the Falkland household directly from Douai where he had gone to study with the Jesuits after renouncing the English church and declaring himself a Catholic. His disenchantment with the Jesuits after but a few months brought him back to the Anglican Church where, after a period of hesitation concerning some details of the Thirty-Nine Articles, he accepted a living. As the godson of William Laud, his religious peregrinations were of some note, and it is unlikely that Hobbes would have failed to become acquainted with him at Great Tews. Aubrey claims Hobbes knew him and quotes Hobbes as saying of Chillingworth, "He was like a lusty fighting fellow that did drive his enemies before him, but would often give his own party smart back-blowes,"[9] a remark that would well fit the *Religion of Protestants*.

Hales was a fellow at Oxford and had acted as an observer for the English with the English ambassador at the Synod of Dort, from which he returned quite disgusted with endless theological disputes over what he considered impenetrable mysteries. He returned to private life and preferring the peaceful role of scholar declined Laud's offer of a living in the church. Whether Hobbes knew him is uncertain, but he maintained a close relationship with both Falkland and Chillingworth and exercised considerable influence on the members of the circle. Hobbes could scarcely have failed to be aware of a man who so impressed his contemporaries that he was inevitably referred to in the writings of the period, and after, as the "ever-memorable Mr. Hales."[10]

In a sermon preached during Easter week 1617 at Oxford, Hales anticipated the doctrines that were to be central in the thought of both Chillingworth and Hobbes on religious matters. Entitled "Concerning the Abuses of Obscure and Difficult Places of Holy Scripture, and Remedies against Them," the sermon was aimed at those who "deal with Scriptures as Chemickes deale with naturall bodies, torturing them to extract that out of them which God and nature never put in them." After exposing the motives which tempt men into exercising their ingenuity on obscurer passages of the Scriptures, Hales expounds what for him are the only sound exegetical canons. There are, he argues, but two "certaine and infallible" interpreters of Scripture, Scripture itself and its author, the Holy Ghost. Scripture can be said to interpret itself when "the wordes & circumstances doe sound unto us the prime, naturall, and principall sense" they carry. In such places the words can be read literally and the message will emerge clearly without any need of interpretation. However, where the Scriptures are "obscure, involved and intricate" or contain "some secret mystery," only the Holy Ghost himself is a competent interpreter.

On both his right and his left Hales had those who would claim to speak with the authority of the Holy Ghost and he does not leave unplugged the opening this last doctrine seems to offer them. According to Hales the Holy Ghost's direct inspiration of men was limited to the original set of Apostles whose function it was to transmit the divine message to all mankind through their preaching and writing. The scriptural promise that men will always be provided with a guiding spirit has thus had a dual mode of fulfillment, one to the Apostles by way of "a private and secret informing of their understandings," and another to all other men by which "what was written by revelation in their [the

Apostle's] hearts, for our instruction have they written in their bookes." Thus a claim neither to the Apostolic succession nor to having been spiritually regenerated provides a basis for claiming infallibility in scriptural interpretation.

So far as the claims of spiritual rebirth are concerned, Hales argues that being filled with the spirit of God "infuses no knowledge of points of faith," nor does it deliver "particular information for resolution in any doubtful case." That was the prerogative of the Apostles. "[T]o us, for information, otherwise than out of these bookes, the spirit speakes not." The spirit of God in regenerating a man does not inform him regarding the tenets of Christianity but merely "stirres up . . . a desire to learn" those things needful for his direction. And for this learning he is directed to "the church and the scriptures."

This last remark cannot be taken as suggesting Hales felt the Anglican Church, any more than the Roman, was a special source of information independent of the Scriptures. Hales's central point limiting the informative action of the Holy Ghost to the Apostles is destructive of all post-Apostolic pretensions to special informative powers whether individual or institutional. The upshot of Hales's argument is that latter-day men are limited for their direction to those plain places where Scripture clearly reveals its meaning. Given this limitation and the scriptural promise of guidance, these plain places must contain all that is necessary for man's salvation. This is confirmed in two rules Hales lays down for scriptural interpretation. The first is that "the litterall, plaine and uncontroversable meaning of Scripture, without any addition or supply by way of interpretation, is that alone which for ground of faith we are necessarily bound to accept, except it bee there where the holy Ghost him selfe treads us out another waie."[11] The second rule directs us regarding obscure places. "In places of ambiguous and doubtfull, or darke and intricate meaning, it is sufficient if we religiously admire and acknowledge and confess. . . ." Or, as Hobbes was to put it, we must "captivate our understanding to the words" (III, 360). Good Christians must found their faith on those doctrines so clearly enunciated in the Scriptures that their meaning is unmistakable. Before those passages less lucid they must humble their wits.

The position sketched in Hales's small sermon forms the core of Chillingworth's immense *Religion of Protestants*. The whole fabric of his discourse, he asserts in the preface, is "naturally deducible out of this one Principle, *that all things necessary to salvation are evidently contain'd in Scripture*." "The way to heaven," Chillingworth insists, was laid out by Christ and the Apostles and "is no narrower now, then [*sic*] Christ left it" (p. 180).[12] By applying our reason to the Scriptures we can discover that way. "Right reason grounded on Divine revelation and common notions, written by God in the hearts of all men, and deducing according to never failing rules of Logick, consequent deductions from them" (preface) will discover the necessary foundations of faith. The man who follows Scripture and reason "in all his opinions and actions, and does not only seeme to doe so, followes alwaies God" (*ibid.*).

Reason discovers two kinds of truths in the Scriptures which it is necessary to believe; those necessary to be believed as essential to salvation and those necessary to believe "not in themselves, but only by accident, because they were written" (p. 22; cf. p. 135). These are distinguished in two ways. First, there is general agreement about those doctrines necessary to salvation, "there being no more certain signe that a Point is not evident than that honest and understanding and indifferent men . . . after mature consideration of the matter differ about it" (preface; cf. p. 41). Thus those men who search the Scriptures sincerely "and not to wrest it to their preconceived Phansies" (p. 58) "may be secure that [they] cannot erre fundamentally. And they that doe so cannot differ in fundamentals. So that notwithstanding their differences . . . the same heaven may receive them all" (p. 23).

The second criterion for distinguishing fundamentals is derived from John 1:4, where men are instructed to "believe not every spirit, but try the spirits whether they be of God." To discover whether a spirit is of God we must "consider whether they *confess Jesus to be the Christ*" (preface). To the test of self-evidence and general agreement, this criterion adds a test of content. The necessary fundamentals of faith will be those that "constitute and make up the covenant between God and man in Christ." The accessories, on the other hand, concern "matters of History, of Prophecy, of mystery, of Policy, of Oeconomie, & such like, which are evidently not intrinsicall to the covenant" (pp. 22–23). A fundamental of faith then will be a doctrine concerning the covenant between God and man laid down in the Scriptures with sufficient clarity that all unbiased readers will agree on its import.

Despite these relatively clear criteria, Chillingworth was not anxious to set down a definitive list of fundamental beliefs. His interest was, at this time, in providing a foundation for Christian unity and he no doubt knew that the construction of such a list could only cause more wrangling. He thus softens his position by suggesting that the same *range* of fundamentals is not required of all men. "God himself hath told us that where much is given much shall be required" (Luke 1:2), Chillingworth argues, and this means men's obligations of belief will vary as do their circumstances and capabilities. "To Infants, Deafe-men, Mad-men," for all we can know, nothing has been given and so "nothing shall be required. Others perhaps may have meanes only given them to believe That God is, and that he is a rewarder of them that seeke him." To these it "shall not be damnable, that they believe only so much." This defines the "*minimum quod sic*, the lowest degree of faith wherewith . . . God will be pleased" (p. 133).

In this spirit of tolerance, Chillingworth is also willing to accept a maximum effort of faith. Should a man not trust himself to apply correctly the criteria necessary for distinguishing fundamentals from accessories, he may escape his task by simply believing all the Scriptures, for, "in believing all that is there, we are sure to believe all that is necessary" (p. 135). In a passage that may well have suggested the pill image to Hobbes, Chillingworth compares the Scriptures to a medicinal compound about which physicians disagree, some telling the patient "that all the ingredients were absolutely necessary; some that only some were necessary, the rest only profitable . . . lastly some, that some only were necessary, some profitable, and the rest superfluous, yet not hurtfull, yet all with one accord in agreeing in this, That the *whole receipt* [*sic*] *had in it all things necessary* for the recovery of his health . . ." (p. 159). The reasonable patient, Chillingworth suggests, will not enter medical school in order to adjudicate the dispute, but simply swallow the whole concoction down and be done with it. Should one, in this wholesale process err on some nonfundamental point, it will not be damnable so long as his attempt was honestly to understand God's meaning. In such cases a man may be said to "believe implicitly even those very truths against which they erre" (p. 18; cf. pp. 92, 157). Strenuous searchings of the Scripture are neither necessary nor advisable. The obscure passages may be accepted for what they are, mysteries, and man may rest assured that "if God's will had been we should have understood him more certainly, he would have spoken more plainly" (p. 83).[13]

By such maneuvers Chillingworth attempts to avoid refueling the fires of controversy he is so anxious to dampen. When speaking of the fundamentals of faith, he shows a preference for a general reference to the covenant between God and man or to the messianic role of Jesus. In the course of a discussion of heresy he reluctantly offers the following tentative list of doctrines that must be believed to escape being a heretic.

If any one should deny that there is a God: that this God is omnipotent, omnificient, good, just, true, merciful, a rewarder of them that seek him, a punisher of them that obstinately offend him: that Jesus Christ is the Sonne of God and the Saviour of the World: that it is he by obedience to whom man must look to be saved: If any man should deny either his Birth, Passion, or Ressurection, or attention, or sitting at the right hand of God: his having all power given him in Heaven and Earth: That it is he whom God hath appointed to judge the quick and the dead: that he shall rise again at the last day: That they which repent shall be sav'd: That they which do not believe and repent shall be damned: If a man should hold that either the keeping of the *Mosaicall* Law is necessary to Salvation: or that Good Works are not [he is guilty of heresy] (pp. 101–102).

Chillingworth is quick to point out that this list is not in any way definitive or necessarily exhaustive. These truths are fundamental only because they were "plainly delivered in Scripture" where they lay open to anyone's unbiased inspection. They are fundamental for this reason only and not because they appear on any list purporting to be authoritative.

The Christocentric doctrine expounded by Chillingworth was not the isolated view of an eccentric but formed the dominant thrust of Anglican thought in the period. At the beginning of the century Hooker had claimed that the "main drift of the whole New Testament" is found in John 20:31: "These things are written, that ye might believe that Jesus is the Christ the Son of God, and that in believing ye might have life through his name." The only difference in the messages of the Old and New Testaments that Hooker finds is in their tense, the Old teaching salvation "through Christ that should come, the New by teaching that Christ is come. . . ."[14] Laud enunciated what he took to be the* *quaedam prima credibilia* "in the bosom of which all other articles [of fundamental faith] lay wrapped and folded up" by citing Hebrews 11:16: "He that comes to God, must believe that he is, and that he is a rewarder of them that seek him" and I John 4:2: "every spirit that confesseth Jesus Christ come in the flesh is of God."[15] In the middle of the century Cudworth affirms that "the Gospel is nothing else but God descending into the world in our form and conversing with us in our likeness, that He might allure and draw us up to God and make us partakers of his divine form."[16] And at the end of the century Robert South without qualification asserts that the only belief necessary to salvation is "Jesus is the Son of God."[17] It is the full acceptance of this doctrine of salvation that forms the core of Hobbes's own religious position and provides the stable point from which he is able to survey and criticize all other facets of religious life.

Before moving to Hobbes it may be useful to blunt the edge of a possible difficulty. It may seem odd to connect Hobbes, whom Pogson Smith called an "Erastian without limits," with Chillingworth and Hales who are justly famous as progenitors of religious toleration in England.[18] But however much their writings may have stimulated the growth of toleration, their position contains a gaping defect as a theoretical foundation for tolerance in religious practice. For nothing follows necessarily for practice from the view that salvation is totally dependent on holding certain fundamental beliefs. Hooker had argued that matters of practice such as the location of the communion table and the ministerial vestment were "things indifferent." One might then argue that these matters could be allowed to vary with taste or disposition. On the other hand, the fundamental unimportance of such practices also undercuts any claim to conscientious objection against such things being regulated by the sovereign. If matters of practice are indifferent, then what can be the motive of those that resist conforming? To those who saw a unified church as providing essential moral support to the civil state, the answer seemed clear enough. Laud, who in matters of doctrine was as moderate as his godson, believed that only a unified church could provide the critical moral underpinning necessary for a peaceful civil state. "It is not possible in any Christian commonwealth that the Church should melt and the State stand firm. For there can be no firmness without law; and no laws can be binding if there be no conscience to obey them; penalty alone could never, can never do it. And no school can teach conscience but the Church of Christ. For wherever you find the Church melt and dissolve, there you shall see conscience decay."[19]

In Laud's mind the function of keeping men's consciences attached to the civil laws could not be fragmented without disaster. Those who attack the unified administration of this function and rail against bishops and uniformity, with no grounds in conscientious fear for their salvation, are but proto-revolutionaries. "They whoever they be, that would overthrow *sedes Ecclesiae*, the 'seats of ecclesiatical government,' will not spare, if ever they get power, to have a pluck at the 'throne of David.' And there is not a man that is for 'parity'—all fellows in the Church—but he is not for monarchy in the State."[20] The result of letting such men have their way would be a chaos as grim as Hobbes's state of nature for when the church melts so does the state.

. . . when it is *terra liquefacta,* when a kingdom "dissolves" and "melts," what then? What? why then no man is in safety until it settles again; not a man. . . . All men then seek what to do; the wisest seek, and the strongest seek; all. And it must needs be so. For so long as a State is *terra,* like solid ground, men know where to set their footing. . . . But when it is once *terra lique- facta,* "molten" and "dissolved," there is no footing, no founda- tion then. . . . All is foul then, and no foundation.[21]

This view of the church performing a critical secular function does not conflict with the doctrine of fundamentals, but can draw positive support from it. As a foundation of the English state began to "liquify," Chillingworth himself became a steadfast sup- porter of his godfather's Erastian policies.[22] Hobbes, then, is not in strange company.

II

Hobbes, no less than Laud, was aware of the way in which fragmented religious authority could undermine the stability of states. While he subjects a wide enough range of religious topics to criticism to be credited with a fully fledged philosophy of religion, his interest in such topics is generally more in their political implications than in the topics themselves. In dealing with religious matters he aims generally to show that they are to be rested securely in the hands of the civil sovereign. Much of his analysis is destructive and skeptical as he attempts to de- stroy the positions of anti-Erastians, but his wasting assaults through the doctrinal and scriptural strongholds of his enemies should not be mistaken as evidence for any personal skepticism or atheism on Hobbes's part. His treatment of religious matters is firmly grounded on his full acceptance of the simplified Chris-

tianity developed by moderate Anglicans like Hales and Chillingworth as can be seen from his accounts of religion, worship, and
salvation.

Religion for Hobbes, as the famous definition of *Leviathan*
makes clear, is a legal organization of certain emotions. "Fear of
power invisible, feigned by the mind, or imagined from tales
publicly allowed, RELIGION; not allowed, SUPERSTITION. And
when the power imagined, is truly such as we imagine, TRUE
RELIGION" (III, 145).

It should be noted that there is nothing skeptical in this definition. True religions are allowed for when the real invisible power
is correctly imagined. And the verb "feigned" here carries the
now archaic sense of "giving fictional representation to" and
distinguishes a creative aspect of the mind from the merely re-
productive activity of imagination. A feigning or imagining
would be necessary, given Hobbes's psychology, for any religion
to have emotional content. Passions are triggered, according to
Hobbes, by the impact of motions associated with "phantasms"
impinging on the vital motions of the body. Hence an invisible
power, or a completely inconceivable one as God is for Hobbes,
would have to be feigned or imagined before any emotional response could occur.

In mentioning this emotional aspect of religion in his definition, Hobbes prepares the way for his fuller account, later in
Leviathan, of the natural history of religion. There he distinguishes four "seeds" of religion, "opinion of ghosts, ignorance
or second causes, devotion towards what men fear, and the taking
of things casual for prognostics" (III, 98). These seeds are not yet
religion. They become religion only when "cultured" by men
and formed in sets of publicly sanctioned beliefs and practices.
Otherwise they remain mere superstitions. Some men have
"nourished and cultured" such seeds purely from their own interests and out of their own imaginations; others, however, have
done so "by God's command and direction" (III, 99). Both true
and false religions, however, serve the same political purpose, "to
make those men that relied on them, the more apt to obedience,

laws, peace, charity, and civil society" (III, 99). Religions then are the outcome of men's attempts to gain a more secure political state by utilizing the natural fear and curiosity of their fellows. That is their natural origin.

Religions *consist*, on the other hand, of civil rules; in the case of true religions, in "rules of honoring God, which we have from the laws" (I, xi). Religion is not to be confused with philosophy which is private opinion arising out of natural reason (I, xi).[23] Hobbes objects strongly to those who would turn religion into an art of scriptural exigesis as, in his opinion, the scholastics had done. "I like not the design of drawing religion into an art, whereas it ought to be a law; and though not the same in all countries, yet in every country indisputable" (*Behemoth*, p. 43). Religions begin in attempts to organize natural fears in the interest of civil peace and issue in sets of rules governing the honoring of God, that is to say in a legally authorized form of worship.

Worship "is an outward act, the sign of inward honor" (II, 210).[24] One may, of course, honor God "in inward thought" by thinking "as highly of his power and goodness as is possible" (III, 348). Such honoring when expressed in outward words or deeds becomes worship and, like all actions, becomes subject to law.

All law for Hobbes has both a natural and a positive part. The natural law of worship prescribes that we speak of God only in those words that "signify honor with all men" such as "the general words of *virtues* and *powers* which cannot be taken in an ill sense" (II, 211).[25] Thus we may say of God that he is good, just, omnipotent, omniscient, and so on. In doing so we do not, cannot mean to describe God, for, according to Hobbes, words do not carry their normal meaning when applied to God. Rather they function as pure honorifics. We merely confess our own "admiration and obedience, which is the property of a mind yielding all the honor it possibly can do" (II, 216).

What words can never be taken in an ill sense depends upon the linguistic conventions adopted by men. "Good," "just," and "wise," for example, are suitable for worship only because as a matter of fact men do use them to refer only to things they esteem. However, the hurly-burly of everyday usage may result in negative connotations becoming attached to any word and so what words are to be held as fit for worship must ultimately be decided by positive law. "The city . . . by right, that is to say, they who have the power of the whole city, shall judge what *names* or *appellations* are more, what less honorable for God; that is to say, what doctrines are to be held and professed concerning the nature of God and his operations" (II, 219).[26] The final say regarding what is to be said in worship rests with the sovereign.

The relationship here between the natural and the positive law of verbal worship is identical with that between natural and positive political laws. In the state of nature, Hobbes argues, all men agree perfectly well that modesty, equity, humanity, and justice are virtues and theft, murder, and adultery are vices. What they cannot agree on is "in what each of them doth consist." Peace then depends upon sovereign decision ending such disputes. Thus the natural laws prescribe at best a certain form which must be given content and applicability by positive law (II, 48, 85–87; III, 355–356; *Elements*, p. 112).[27]

This same relationship holds regarding worshipful actions. Natural reason can identify three classes of action which as such signify an intention of honoring; obedience, thanksgiving, and prayers (II, 211; III, 349). Here again what is to constitute such actions is generally a matter for civil decision. Hobbes's sense of the possible fails him here and he asserts that some actions, unlike words, "signify not by men's appointments, but naturally; even as effects are signs of their causes." To discover "the body's uncleanness," he suggests, is always a sign of scorn while to "draw near and discourse decently and humbly" or "to give way or to yield in any matter of private benefit" are always signs of honor (II, 219–220; III, 356). Beyond these few, however, lie an "infinite number" of actions such as "in saluting to be bareheaded, to put off the shoes, to bend the body . . . forms of ceremony, and the like" which are honorable only by custom or decree.

Any attempt by a man publicly to worship God through privately determined prayers or actions would, by Hobbes's definition, fail. Since worship is an *outward sign* of honor, the signifying fails if the sign is not generally recognized. "A sign is not a sign to him that giveth it, but to him to whom it is made, that is to the spectator." While a man might worship in isolation by private signs, he *cannot* successfully do so "in the sight of the multitude. . . . For if to them the words, or actions by which we intend honor, seem ridiculous and tending to contumely, they are no worship because no signs of honor" (III, 350).

The upshot of Hobbes's treatment of religion and worship is that there may be diverse forms of true established religions. So long as what men say and do in honoring God is publicly recognized, they truly worship God. This open view of religion is not predicated on any arch-skepticism, but on the view Hobbes shared with his Anglican contemporaries that the road to heaven was broad and the essence of Christianity simple. If salvation is a matter of believing a few simple and clear doctrines, then matters of religious practice are for the most part, as Hooker put it, "things indifferent."

Hobbes, while he does not press the point, develops, as did his Anglican contemporaries, the foundation for what they frequently called their "charity" toward members of other communions. The Anglicans commonly held that so long as an individual embraced those fundamental beliefs definitive of Christianity they would be saved regardless of the errors of the religion they practiced.[28] Hobbes first publicly adopted the moderate Anglican's doctrine of salvation and Christianity in the *Elements of Law* which began to circulate in manuscript just two years after *The Religion of Protestants* had seen its first two editions. As we noted above this doctrine is the fixed center from which Hobbes's explorations of other religious questions radiate.

Hobbes's claim that absolute subjection to a sovereign was a necessary condition of civil peace faced a strong objection from Christians who held that the Scriptures were God's revealed directions to salvation and eternal life. Surely, it would be argued, the commands of the civil authority may conflict with the prescriptions of God's word and the conscientious Christian cannot be under an absolute obligation to follow fallible men rather than God himself. This argument, Hobbes mentions, is of recent origin and arises now among "those Christians only, to whom it is allowed to take for the sense of Scripture that which they make thereof, either by their own private interpretation, or by the interpretation of such as are not called thereunto by public authority" (*Elements*, p. 145).

Hobbes begins by pointing out that civil law does not bind or govern man's conscience "unless it break out into action either of the tongue or other part of the body" (*Elements*, p. 146). The important question then is not what a man may believe in his own bosom, but what actions would necessarily imply a denial of that faith necessary for salvation. To identify such actions we must first identify the necessary and fundamental elements of a saving faith. Now the core of Christianity is the belief in the Christhood of Jesus. The essential element of faith required for salvation is belief in Jesus together with whatever other beliefs are logically necessary for this core doctrine to be true. The only command a sincere Christian might be conscientiously entitled to disobey would be to deny directly one of these beliefs. Living under a Christian prince, a Christian has nothing to fear and no cause for disobedience, for no Christian sovereign will require his subjects to deny Christ. A Christian living under an infidel prince might, however, find himself faced with such a demand. The ordinary Christian may then avail himself of the precedent of Naaman and outwardly conform while inwardly denying the significance of his action, and be reassured knowing that acts done in obedience to lawful commands are not properly his acts but those of the commander's. In the case of one whose special calling is to be a witness to Christ there is no choice but to "go to Christ by martyrdom" (II, 316). To those who find this a hard saying, Hobbes replies that "he that is not glad of any just occasion of martyrdom, has not the faith he professeth, but pretends it only . . ." (III, 601–602).

Hobbes separates the "fundamentals" from "superstructions" by sorting out those doctrines declared by Christ and the Apostles to be necessary to salvation from those which have been objects of disputes among later Christians (*Elements*, p. 148). The central of these is, of course, the proposition "Jesus is the Christ." The remainder of the fundamentals consists of explications of this proposition and its logical implications. In the first group are such propositions as Jesus "is God's anointed . . . that he was the true and lawful king of Israel, the Son of David; the Saviour of the world." Four basic beliefs make up the "evident" implications of the fundamental tenet: "belief in God the Father . . . belief in God the Holy Ghost . . . belief of the Scriptures by which we believe those points, and of the immortality of the soul, without which we cannot believe he is a saviour." These fundamentals then constitute all the beliefs "essential to the calling of a Christian" (*Elements*, pp. 148–149).[29]

This identification of the fundamentals of Christian faith is supported by a series of considerations by now familiar from our account of Hobbes's Anglican predecessors (*Elements*, pp. 149–153; II, 307–313; III, 591–96). Like Hooker, Hobbes argues in the first place that the scope and evident intent of all the writings of the Apostles, whether in the Gospels or in the sermons written after Christ's life on earth had ended, are to establish Jesus as the Messiah. Secondly, like Chillingworth, Hobbes argues that "Christ's yoke is easy and his burthen light" (Matt. 11:30). If not how could little children or the good thief or Paul on the road to Damascus be saved so suddenly and without benefit of a religion? If all the arcane doctrines debated by sectaries and theologians and all the complexities of worship now practiced were required for salvation, Hobbes says with point, "there would be nothing in the world so hard as to be a Christian." And that, he insists, is not the case. With Chillingworth, Hobbes asserts that "there is no more faith required for salvation in one man than in another" (*Elements*, p. 152).

Finally Hobbes clinches his case by what, although he calls them "arguments," are nothing more than straightforward presentations of places in Scripture where the fundamentals he has identified are plainly asserted to be necessary foundations of Christian faith. Hobbes here eschews interpretation of the passages he cites, relying on "the evident testimonies of Holy Writ." Like Hales and Chillingworth he believes the message of such passages to be clear and unambiguous, "let who will be the interpreter" (II, 307n, 312).[30] As Hobbes says in *Behemoth*, "All that is required both in faith and in manners for man's salvation is . . . set down in Scriptures as plainly as can be" (p. 54).

With regard to those places which are obscure, "allegorical and difficult," Hobbes is again at one with Hales and Chillingworth. It is simply not the business of human reason to penetrate mysteries of Scripture. Through reason we gain scientific knowledge, through faith we gain salvation. Scientific knowledge is of causal relations, but since God is uncaused there can be no science of God or of things divine. In *De Cive*, in a passage that was the parent to the one discussed in the first section of this paper, Hobbes distinguishes the differing manners in which propositions of faith and knowledge are to be received. Knowledge is analytic and "deliberately takes a proposition broken and chewed"; faith on the other hand "swallows it down whole and entire." "The only way to *know,*" Hobbes believes, "is by definition" (II, 305). But for matters of faith "which exceed human capacity and are propounded to be believed" attempts at analytical definition and explication only render them "more obscure and harder to credit." The wholesome pill chewed is bitterer and more difficult to retain.

Once more, Hobbes follows Chillingworth in holding that men who are tempted into false beliefs in the course of trying to reason out the sense of obscure passages may still be saved so long as they continue to believe the fundamentals. "Whatsoever is necessary for them to know, is so easy, as not to need interpretation," Hobbes insists, and "whatsoever is more does them no good" (*Behemoth*, p. 55). Nor do such undigested ingredients of faith do any harm so long as men are not tempted by them into meddling with the sovereign prerogatives.

III

The account above of the doctrines of Hobbes, Hales, and Chill-ingworth regarding the fundamentals of faith is brief and, in some minor matters, incomplete. It is, however, sufficient to allow us to draw a few conclusions with a degree of confidence. First it seems clear that Hobbes's view of salvation, and indeed of Christianity, was substantially identical with that held by leading Anglican thinkers in the first decades of the century. Given the close relationship between Hobbes and the Falkland circle, it is not unlikely that Hobbes's views were directly influenced by Chillingworth. Certainly this simplified Christianity, which made salvation depend on accepting but a small number of propositions clearly laid down in Scripture and at the same time dismissing the obscure ranges of theology as inessential, must have been congenial and welcome to the mind of a man like Hobbes, enthralled as he was with the success of the new scientific approach and anxious to extend it to the problems of politics. For this doctrine, as we have seen, simultaneously provided security for the soul and freedom for the critical exercise of reason. Piety is isolated from ceremonies and theologies, and science is left free to expose the absurdities and civil dangers that result when such things are given too much weight in private conscience. This is not to suggest that Hobbes embraced the Anglican doctrine out of convenience, but only to point out the natural attraction of such a doctrine for him. With this view of Christianity he could follow Bacon's maxim of rendering unto faith what was faith's and simultaneously encompass the problems of society within a scientific system.

Secondly, noting the wedge this doctrine drives between personal piety and the traditional trappings and interests of religion makes it possible to reconcile Hobbes's steadfast assertions of belief both with his skeptical assaults on traditional religious ideas and doctrines and with his changing interpretations of many of these latter matters, without having recourse to theories about Hobbes's sincerity or lack of it. Strauss, who is fond of finding secret doctrines peeping between the lines of texts, noting Hobbes's changing interpretations of many religious questions from the *Elements* to *Leviathan*, and quite overlooking the significance of the consistently stated doctrine of salvation, confidently asserts what he terms Hobbes's "unbelief" and suggests that the changes are the result of a studied, self-interested expediency. In particular he notes that in the *Elements* Hobbes defends an episcopal form of church governance and in *Leviathan* rejects this in favor of independentism.[31] Strauss then remarks that "Hobbes kept pace in his way—which was not very edifying —with the development from Anglican Episcopalianism to Independentism. . . ."[32] But certainly the existence of such changes does not support the charge that Hobbes was a nonbeliever or that there was anything particularly unedifying about the changes. So long as the doctrines in question did not affect the core of fundamental beliefs which constituted his personal piety, Hobbes was perfectly free to change his opinions on them as he saw fit. Hobbes's comments on independentism in *Leviathan* seem to reflect a growing awareness of the rights of individual conscience that is perfectly consistent with his own doctrine of salvation.[33] But whether this is the case or not, at least Hobbes is being consistent with his own view of the subject's proper duty in accepting that form of church governance under Cromwell. And if this was done out of self-interest, nothing in his own ideals forbade such prudent accommodations.

If Hobbes was not an atheist then, one might very well wonder why his contemporaries so uniformly took him to be one. While this problem constitutes another study which cannot be undertaken here, the question demands at least a partial answer. As Skinner has pointed out, those who would theologize Hobbes's politics are committed to a kind of historical absurdity, namely, that all Hobbes's contemporary commentators "entirely missed the point Hobbes was concerned to make, although it was a point they were highly attuned to see; all of them saw instead the opposite point, although none was attuned to do so, and although Hobbes was not in fact making such a point at all."[34] I would suggest that the explanation lies first in the fact that Hobbes's philosophic work is *a*-theistic. The simplified essentialist Christianity which he held sharply separated faith from reason and isolated piety from theology. Such a view left Hobbes completely free to construct a metaphysics, a psychology, and a politics in which the idea of God played no functional role and in which the traditional religious issues could be subjected to the severest criticism and finally left in the hands of the secular ruler. To his religiously attuned contemporaries, Hobbes's system would seem to be the product of an atheistic mind. But that was their mistake; we needn't repeat it.

Secondly, we cannot overlook the effect of Hobbes's insistence that whatever existed was body, including God himself. To the minds of his contemporaries this meant materialism and materialism meant atheism. After all when Vorstius was appointed to a chair at the University of Leyden, James I was incensed enough to intervene across the channel and insist on his dismissal, for he had debased God's purity by "assigning Him a material body, confining His immensity, as not being everywhere, shaking His immutability . . ." and so on.[35] These two factors, the lack of involvement of Hobbes's piety in his philosophy and his insistence on a single substance, body, could easily combine to make his contemporaries uniformly read him as an atheist.

Piety, Hobbes thought, consisted in two things, honoring God in one's heart and signifying that honor by one's words and deeds (IV, 257). Perhaps the quality of that piety can be no better summed up than in Hobbes's own version of the life deserving of salvation presented at the end of his verse *Historia Ecclesia*:

> Our Saviour calls the Man completely blest,
> Whose unaspiring Thoughts few Cares molest,
> His Conscience calm, tho' in low Estate,
> Who envies not the Splendor of the Great;
> By Nature mild, not to fierce Anger prone,
> Who craves no other's Rights, but keeps his own;
> Can view his Neighbor's Wealth, with harmless Eyes,
> Nor wish for Gold, which in his Treas'ry lyes;

Who strives with all his Might, the Paths to tread,
   Which Saints have shewn, and the Messiah led;
Who can his secret Sins, with Tears, lament,
   Reject the Tempter, and in Truth repent,
Whose Heart is clean, whose Soul is free from stain,
   Whose Morals just, and whose Religion's plain;
Who seeks contending Parties to unite,
   Who sows no Scandel, nor provokes to Fight;
Who from his Heart, his Brother's Faults forgives,
   And with no worldly Woes, nor Losses grieves;
Who ne'er at Heaven's imparted Hand repines,
   But his whole Will to God's Decree resigns:
Lastly, who leaves his Load of Crimes behind,
   To Justice, Mercy, and to Grace inclined;
His Soul from Fear of Hellish Rage shall save,
   Whose Sins are sunk in His *Redeemer's Grave.*[36]

These lines, while earning Hobbes no great credit as a poet, express a credo which is consistent with what we know of his life and with his expressed views on salvation, religion, and citizenship. By his own lights Hobbes, I think, was a pious man. But it is clear that the nature of piety as Hobbes understood it is personal, and in no way connected with systems of worship, systems of theology, or systems of scientific knowledge. And so there is no conflict between Hobbes the pious believer and Hobbes the author of a completely naturalistic science of body, man, and societies.

Notes and Selected Bibliography

NOTES

The Motivation of Hobbes's Political Philosophy

1. *The Divine Right of Kings* and *From Gerson to Grotius.*
2. *Divine Right of Kings*, p. 11.
3. *Ibid.*, p. 221. Technically, discussions centered on the nature of *Jus.* The ambiguity of Jus, meaning both command and law on one side, and right, on the other side, has been frequently noted. At this time, it was not so much ambiguity which existed as two sides of one notion. Jus is primarily *authority*, and secondarily *authorization*, depending, of course, upon authority.
4. *Ibid.*, p. 219.
5. See, for example, the quotations from royalist writers, Falkner and Filmer, in *ibid.*, pp. 388–389.
6. Quoted by Tönnies in *Archiv für Geschichte der Philosophie* (1890), p. 223.
7. Now published (from manuscript) by Tönnies under the title of *The Elements of Law Natural and Politic* (London, 1889).
8. William Molesworth, ed., *The English Works of Thomas Hobbes* IV (London, 1839; first published, 1655), 414. References to the *Works* will hereafter be cited in the text by volume and page numbers.
9. Tönnies's edition, p. 75. See also pp. 63, 57, 49, 95, 172, etc.
10. *Ibid.*, pp. 2–3.
11. Quoted by Tönnies in *Archiv*, XVII, 302. See also *Works*, IV, 407.
12. Harrington, on the contrary, who was a genuinely democratic writer with an interest which was modern, economic, and secular, in differing radically from Hobbes as to respective merits of royal and popular government, says, "In most other things I believe Mr. Hobbes is, and in future ages will be, accounted the best writer in this day in the world."
13. Quoted from Ritchie, *Natural Rights*, p. 9. He quotes from the preface of Firth to the *Clarke Papers.*
14. Lawson, *An Examination of the Political Part of Mr. Hobbes, His Leviathan*, pp. 96, 123, 127. When one considers the prevalence of this idea of the duty of private

judgment, one is almost inclined to align Hobbes's criticism of it with that passed by Auguste Comte upon Protestantism.

15. *Ibid.*, pp. 133–134. Italics mine.

16. As Hobbes saw, this doctrine is either a negation of sovereignty or works out practically (as it has done so largely in this country) in placing the judges in the seat of sovereignty—a "government of lawyers, not of men," to paraphrase the old saying. Locke comes close to this legal position, and historically is half way between Hobbes's location of sovereignty and Rousseau's ascription of sovereignty to the legislative body alone.

17. Figgis, *Divine Right of Kings*, p. 229. See his note for references in support of the text.

18. See also *Works*, VI, 194–195.

19. In the *Leviathan* (*Works*, III, 256), he criticizes this definition of Coke's on the ground that long study only increases error unless the foundations are true and agreed upon.

20. *Hobbes* (London, 1886), p. 57.

21. See also *Works*, II, xxii, in which he says that there is only one point not *demonstrated* in the whole book—namely, the superior commodiousness of monarchy; for, as we must remember, Hobbes always means mathematical method by demonstration.

22. Tönnies, *Archiv*, p. 69.

23. I think that there is more than a shadowy reminiscence of Hobbes in Locke's contention that morals and mathematics are the two demonstrative subjects. What we "make ourselves" and general notions which, being the "workmanship of the understanding," are their own archetypes, are not, after all, far apart.

24. *Works*, VI, 213, 236; III, 330; VII, 345; III, 713. See also IV, 204.

25. *Works*, III, 713, for his suggestion to Cromwell to have his doctrines taught in the universities; see *ibid.*, VII, 343–352, for a defense of the proposal.

26. In his dedication to the Earl of Newcastle, dated in 1640, where men's agreement in mathematics, due to dependence on reason, is contrasted with their controversies and contradictions in policy and justice, due to their following passion.

27. Compare with this the following from the *Leviathan*: "For all men are by nature provided with notable multiplying glasses, that is, their passions and self-love, through which, every little payment appeareth a great grievance; but are destitute of those prospective glasses, namely, moral and civil science, to see afar off the miseries that hang over them, and can not without such payments be avoided" (III, 170).

28. They are called laws only metaphorically, since only a command is a law. But in the sense in which the faculty of reason is a gift of God, and God may be said to command us to act rationally, they are true laws or commands.

29. In his own day, Hobbes had logically the benefit of the fact that "self-preservation" was laid down by practically all writers as the first article of the law of nature. Moral laws are "eternal" to Hobbes in exactly the same way as are geometrical propositions. They flow from original definitions whose subjects include their predicates in such a way that the latter cannot be denied without falling, at some point, into formal self-contradiction. The absolute "obligation" which the subject is under not to withdraw from the compact by which he entered the State is the obligation not to contradict his own premises.

30. Hobbes never attributes physical omnipotence to the sovereign, but only a power to threaten and to enforce threats which arouses enough fear to influence

men's outer conduct. His whole position very closely resembles that of Kant regarding the relation of the moral and the legal, much as the two differ in their conception of the moral.

31. *Leviathan*, pt. II, chap. XXX. Vol. III, chap. XIII, "Concerning the Duties of Them That Rule." See also vol. IV, *De Corpore Politico*, chap. IX, which sets out from the proposition, "This is the general law for sovereigns, that they procure, to the uttermost of their endeavour, the good of the people."

32. It is in the same vein when Hobbes says that rebellion is not an offense against the civil law, but against the moral or natural law, for they violate the obligation to obedience which is before all civil law—since the institution of civil law depends upon it (*Works*, II, 200).

33. Compare the *Leviathan*, III, 335.

The *Philosophia Prima* of Thomas Hobbes

1. Thomas Hobbes, "The Author's Epistle to the Reader," p. xiii, in *Elements of Philosophy: The First Section, Concerning Body*, vol. I of *The English Works of Thomas Hobbes*, ed. William Molesworth (London, 1839; first published, 1655). References to this volume of the *Works* will hereafter be cited in the text by part, chapter, section, and page numbers.

2. Harold Höffding, *A History of Modern Philosophy*, I (Eng. trans., N.Y.: Dover, 1955), 264.

3. Frithiof Brandt, *Thomas Hobbes's Mechanical Conception of Nature* (Eng. trans., Copenhagen: Levin & Munksgaard, 1928; Danish original, 1921), p. 340.

4. Höffding, *History of Modern Philosophy*, I, 264–271.

5. Leo Strauss, *The Political Philosophy of Hobbes: Its Basis and Genesis*, trans. Elsa M. Sinclair (Oxford: Clarendon Press, 1936).

6. W. H. Greenleaf, "Hobbes: The Problem of Interpretation," in ed. Reinhart Koselleck and Roman Schnur *Hobbes-Forschungen* (Berlin: Duncker & Humblot, 1969), pp. 9–31. This collection is excellent and includes a bibliography of Hobbes studies *im deutschen Sprachraum*. This collection is the proceedings of an international Hobbes colloquium held at Ruhr University, 1967.

7. Arrigo Pacchi, "Cinquant'anni di studi hobbesiani," *Rivista di filosofia*, LVII (1966), 306–335. See also his *Convenzione e ipotesi nella formazione della filosofia naturale di Thomas Hobbes* (Florence: La Nuova Italia, 1965), reviewed in *Journal of the History of Philosophy*, VI (1968), 83–85, by Herbert W. Schneider. Pacchi says that the *De Corpore* must be reevaluated as a contribution to natural philosophy. He finds that the *philosophia prima* was the result of several attempts at a logic of discovery and culminated in 1655 in a theoretical structure for scientific inquiry based on the interpretation of universals as conventions (not hypotheses). Pacchi regards his final acceptance of the "convention" theory in his *Leviathan* (1651) as being the result of its agreement with his political covenant theory.

8. J. W. N. Watkins, *Hobbes's System of Ideas* (London: Hutchinson, 1965); Manfred Riedel, "Zum Verhältnis von Ontologie und politischen Theorie bei Hobbes," in *Hobbes-Forschungen*, pp. 103–118.

9. An early essay became chap. XLVI of *Leviathan*, "Of Darkness from Vain Philosophy and Fabulous Traditions." Oakeshott edition (Oxford: Basil Blackwell, 1960), p. 435. References to *Leviathan* will hereafter be cited in the text by page number.

10. This follows after the passage cited at the beginning.

11. Thomas Spence published his translation as *The Art of Logick* (London, 1628). Hobbes was in the Puritan-influenced Magdalen College, Oxford, from

1603 to 1608, the period when Ramus's logic was replacing school logics in England. The evidence for Ramus's influence on Hobbes is circumstantial, but nevertheless substantial. The same is true of Hobbes's use of Ramist elements in Bacon's logic.

12. Hobbes does not use the word *mechanics*; it has been supplied by historians.

13. Cf. pp. 260–266 where he discusses "the signification of 'spirit.' "

14. *An Answer to a Book Published by Dr. Bramhall* . . . in *Works*, VII, 309ff.

15. *Ibid.*, p. 310.

16. Brandt, *Hobbes's Mechanical Conception of Nature*, pp. 263ff. Brandt has suggested that Hobbes uses "magnitude" here as we might use "mass": it takes on dimensionality and spatiality, but cannot be reduced to them.

17. As Riedel, "Zum Verhältnis," writes: "Im Prozess des Werdens bilden *hyle* und *eidos* auf der einen, *eidos* und *steresis* auf der anderen Seite eine untrennbare Einheit, deren Grund die *physis* ist. . . . Die Natur ist als Werden selbst ein Weg zur Natur" (p. 111).

18. It is misleading to regard this analysis as merely a reworking of Aristotle's "causes," since he reads into them general ideas foreign to Aristotle.

19. Note that his entire reconstruction of the concept of actualization is dyadic, symmetrical, and retrospective (not timeless). Thus *telos* may be *in* nature by way of art, but it is not there *by* nature.

20. Watkins, *Hobbes's System of Ideas*, pp. 121ff, especially chap. VII, "Liberty." Concerning Hobbes's introduction of the concept of endeavor, Watkins writes: "No part of his system has been so undervalued. This may be because a really sharp statement of the theory was difficult without the concepts of differential calculus, of which Hobbes had only certain anticipatory glimmerings. But the main reason for the relative neglect of his theory is that Hobbes signally failed to advertise its importance. . . . Had Hobbes presented it, as he could justifiably have done, as a solution of Descartes' problems, it would surely have been eagerly examined." My treatment here of "endeavor" owes a considerable debt to Professor Watkins.

21. Hobbes summarizes eleven such principles (pt. LL, chap. XV, sec. 1, pp. 203–206). Regarding civil philosophy, see *Leviathan*, pt. II, chap. IV, sec. 1.

22. "Exposition" and "number," i.e., ostensive and quantitative descriptions, are the only two ways of communicating the concept of "magnitude."

23. Cf. *Leviathan*, p. 31.

24. *Ibid.*

Hobbes on the Generation of a Public Person

1. Theodore Waldman, "Hobbes on Liberty: A Study in Constructive Scepticism," in *Proceedings of the Seventh Inter-American Congress of Philosophy*, II (Quebec: University of Laval, 1968), 304–312.

2. William Molesworth, ed., *The English Works of Thomas Hobbes*, I (London, 1839; first published, 1655), viii–ix. References to the *Works* will hereafter be cited in the text by volume and page numbers.

3. Oliver Lawson Dick, ed., *Aubrey's Brief Lives* (Ann Arbor: University of Michigan Press, 1962), p. 133.

4. William Harvey, *On the Motion of the Heart and Blood in Animals*, trans. and ed. Alex. Bowie with an introduction by Mark Graubard (Chicago: Regnery, 1962), pp. 26–27, 85, 136.

5. *Ibid.*, p. 26–27.

6. *Ibid.*, p. 85.

7. *Ibid.*, pp. 116–117.
8. All of chap. VI.
9. It is not until chap. XVI of *Leviathan* (*Works*, III, 147–152) that he turned to a theory of authorization or representation to rectify some of the difficulties present in his earlier works, *The Elements of Law* and *Philosophical Rudiments* (*De Cive*), regarding the transference of power necessary for the institution of a commonwealth.
10. This use is discussed by J. Howard Warrender in *The Political Philosophy of Hobbes: His Theory of Obligation* (Oxford: Clarendon Press, 1957).
11. I have discussed this point briefly in my review of J. H. Warrender's book mentioned in note 10 above. (See *Journal of Philosophy*, LVII, no. 17, August 18, 1960, 559–570.) He had held that Hobbes provided for the establishment of a sovereign by means of transference of right. To support his own thesis, Warrender claimed that this engendered a weak sovereign who was party to the covenant. The argument in this paper is in disagreement with that of Warrender's on these points.
12. Chap. XV of *Leviathan* is a very important chapter and requires close reading. Hobbes's statement and interpretation of these laws is a remarkable insight into the conditions for peace and the responsibilities of government as well as subjects. The sense in which they apply to all men obviously makes them pertinent to men and governors, but, in an impressive way they form the basis for a new concept of commonwealth in modern history. Not only is commonwealth generated by transference and authorization of rights and powers by its subjects but its very subtance and moral basis occur in the statement of the laws of nature.
13. Harvey, *On the Motion of the Heart and Blood in Animals*, especially chaps. XIII and XV.

The Piety of Hobbes

1. In his *True Religion* Milton refers to "an inward and far surpassing light," and "regeneration" is described as a new birth or "renovation" when God "infuses from above new and supernatural faculties into the mind of the renovated." In *Samson Agonistes*, he writes: "He who receives light from above, from the fountain of light, no other doctrine needs, though granted true" (iv, 288).

Hobbes's Anglican Doctrine of Salvation

1. D. Krook, *Three Traditions of Moral Thought* (Cambridge: At the University Press, 1959), chap. IV; F. C. Hood, *The Divine Politics of Thomas Hobbes* (Oxford: Clarendon Press, 1964).
2. These are carefully examined by Quentin Skinner in his review of Hood, "Hobbes's 'Leviathan,'" *Historical Journal*, VII (1964), and, more generally, in "Meaning and Understanding in the History of Ideas," *History and Theory*, VIII (1969). It is to an earlier unpublished version of this paper that I owe the immediately following point.
3. All references to Hobbes are to William Molesworth, ed. *The English Works of Thomas Hobbes* (London, 1839; first published, 1655), with two exceptions; references to *The Elements of Law* (cited as *Elements*) and to *Behemoth* will be to the revised editions prepared by M. M. Goldsmith (New York: Barnes and Noble, 1969). Hereafter references to Hobbes's works will be cited in the text.
4. Sir Leslie Stephen, *Hobbes* (Ann Arbor: University of Michigan Press, 1961),

p. 234; Anthony Flew, "Hobbes," in *A Critical History of Western Philosophy* (London: Collier-Macmillan, 1964), p. 169; Croom Robertson, *Hobbes* (London, 1886), p. 157; Richard Peters, *Hobbes* (Baltimore: Penguin Books, 1956), p. 247.

5. Matters could become extremely crude in the heat of controversy as witness Hobbes's remark in closing his *Considerations upon the Reputation, Loyalty, Manners, and Religion of Thomas Hobbes* (note "Manners") where he blasts his antagonist's writing as being "all error and railing, that is, stinking wind: such as a jade lets fly, when he is too hard girt upon a full belly."

6. Quoted by Paul Elmer More in his useful essay "The Spirit of Anglicanism," introducing P. E. More and F. L. Cross, eds., *Anglicanism: The Thought and Practice of the Church of England, Illustrated from the Religious Literature of the Seventeenth Century* (London: S.P.C.K., 1962), p. xxviii.

7. A detailed account of the circle may be found in Kenneth Murdock, *The Sun at Noon* (New York: Macmillan, 1939), especially chap. V, "Thinking Fools," an appellation awarded the circle by its detractors.

8. According to W. K. Jordan the book saw two editions in the year of its publication (1638) and eleven more in the next hundred years. *The Development of Religious Toleration in England, 1603–1640* (Gloucester, Mass.: Peter Smith, 1965), p. 380n.

9. Oliver Lawson Dick, ed., *Aubrey's Brief Lives* (Ann Arbor: University of Michigan Press, 1962), p. 64.

10. Cf. Jordan, *Development of Religious Toleration*, pp. 400–402; and W. Haller, *The Rise of Puritanism* (New York: Harper, 1957), pp. 242ff.

11. The intent of the final clause, which superficially appears to contradict the position Hales is so carefully constructing, is probably to allow for the Holy Ghost to reassume its informative activities if it so chose. The thought is similar to Sir Thomas Browne's on miracles; they have ceased not because "God cannot, but He will not" any longer perform them.

12. Parenthetical references are to the 1638 first edition in the Huntington Library.

13. The above does not quite exhaust the latitude of belief that Chillingworth accepts. It is not even necessary, he argues, to believe the Scriptures or that they are the word of God. It is sufficient if one believes the central *message* of the Scriptures regardless of the vehicle by which it has been communicated.

14. *Laws of Ecclesiastical Polity*, I, xiv, 4.

15. *A Relation of the Conference between William Laud . . . and Mr. Fisher, the Jesuite*, 1639. This is Laud's only major doctrinal work. Citations (hereafter *Conf.*) will be to vol. II of Laud's *Works* in the Anglo-Catholic Library of 1849. The passage quoted is on p. 50.

16. "Mr. Cudworth's Sermon Preached before the House of Commons at Westminster March 31, 1647," excerpt in *Anglicanism*, p. 783.

17. Quoted by More, "Spirit of Anglicanism," p. xxv.

18. At least one contemporary Catholic apologist, Philip Scot, saw them as a common enemy in his tract "A Treatise of the Schism of England, Wherein Particularly Mr. Hales and Mr. Hobbes Are Modestly Assaulted" (Amsterdam, 1650). In the body of the tract Chillingworth is as frequently (and as modestly) assaulted as Hobbes and Hales.

19. "Sermon for King Charles' First Parliament," Anglo-Catholic Library, *Works*, I, 112.

20. "Sermon before King Charles' Second Parliament," *Works*, I, 83.

21. "Sermon for King Charles' First Parliament," p. 97.

22. For an account of this development see Robert Orr's *Reason and Authority:*

The Thought and Life of William Chillingworth (Oxford: Clarendon Press, 1967), chap. VII.

23. Cf. *Works*, VII, 5. "Religion is not philosophy but law."
24. Cf. *Works*, III, 348, 647.
25. Cf. *ibid.*, p. 349.
26. Cf. *ibid.*, pp. 355–356. By this move Hobbes brings not only worship but the whole of theology under the wing of the sovereign.
27. This statement of the relation of natural and positive law in Hobbes is at best a rough approximation which I hope to fill in at a later date. It might be objected here that if the virtues mentioned in the natural laws have no set meanings, they cannot provide any limitations whatever on sovereign legislation. I would argue that the first two natural laws in Hobbes's lists are free of the semantic relativity infecting the rest and serve as guidelines for the determinations of the sovereign. But this complex matter cannot be explored here.
28. Such liberal notions scandalized both Catholics and Puritans. The puritan Cheynell, Chillingworth's first biographer and deathbed companion, was distressed when Chillingworth in his moribund state refused to recant his view that even Turks, Papists, and Socinians might be saved. See *Chillingworth Novissima, or the Sickness, Heresy, Death and Burial of Mr. Chillingworth*, sec. C; cited by Orr, *Reason and Authority*, p. 185. Laud held a similar open position: cf. *Conf.*, pp. 331ff.
29. See *Works*, II, 307n, where a fuller list, substantially identical with that of Chillingworth's given above, is presented; and *Works*, III, 597–598.
30. See also *Works*, III, 590, where Hobbes rests his case on "places . . . as are without obscurity," and p. 596 where he distinguishes passages that are "plain and easy to understand" from those that are "allegorical and difficult."
31. Leo Strauss, *The Political Philosophy of Hobbes* (Oxford: Clarendon Press, 1936), pp. 71–76. For Hobbes see *Elements*, pp. 163–164; *Works*, III, 696.
32. Strauss, *Political Philosophy of Hobbes*, p. 74.
33. ". . . there ought to be no power over the consciences of men, but of the Word itself, working faith in everyone. . . ." *Works*, III, 696.
34. Skinner, "Hobbes's 'Leviathan,' " p. 22.
35. Quoted by Jordan, *Development of Religious Toleration*, pp. 335–336, from Fuller, *Church History*, V, 413.
36. Quoted from an anonymous English translation printed in London in 1722 under the title "A True Ecclesiastical History from Moses to the Time of Martin Luther."

RECENT STUDIES OF HOBBES: A SELECTED BIBLIOGRAPHY

New Editions (in Chronological Order)

Behemoth or The Long Parliament, ed. Ferdinand Tönnies, prepared and intro. M. M. Goldsmith. 2nd ed. New York: Barnes & Noble, 1969.

The Elements of Law, ed. Ferdinand Tönnies, prepared and intro. M. M. Goldsmith. 2nd ed. New York: Barnes & Noble, 1969.

A Dialogue between a Philosopher and a Student of the Common Laws of England, ed. and intro. Joseph Cropsey. Chicago: University of Chicago Press, 1971.

Man and Citizen, ed. Bernard Gert. Includes a new translation of part of Hobbes's *De Homine* by Charles T. Wood, some of it in English for the first time, and Hobbes's own translation of his *De Cive*. Garden City, N.Y.: Doubleday, 1972.

Books since 1957 (in Chronological Order)

Warrender, Howard. *The Political Philosophy of Hobbes: His Theory of Obligation*. Oxford: Clarendon Press, 1957.

MacPherson, C. B. *The Political Theory of Possessive Individualism: Hobbes to Locke*. Oxford: Clarendon Press, 1962.

Mintz, S. I. *The Hunting of Leviathan: Seventeenth Century Reactions to the Materialism and Moral Philosophy of Thomas Hobbes*. Cambridge: At the University Press, 1962.

Hood, F. C. *The Divine Politics of Thomas Hobbes: An Interpretation of Leviathan*. Oxford: Clarendon Press, 1964.

Pacchi, Arrigo. *Convenzione e ipotesi nella formazione della filosofia naturale di Thomas Hobbes*. Florence: La Nuova Italia, 1965.

Watkins, J. W. N. *Hobbes's System of Ideas*. London: Hutchinson, 1965.

Goldsmith, M. M. *Hobbes's Science of Politics*. New York: Columbia University Press, 1966.

McNeilly, F. S. *The Anatomy of Leviathan*. New York: St. Martin's Press, 1968.

Förster, Winfried. *Thomas Hobbes und der Puritanismus: Grundlagen und Grundfragen seiner Staatslehre.* Berlin: Duncker & Humblot, 1969.
Gauthier, David P. *The Logic of the Leviathan.* Oxford: Clarendon Press, 1969.
Gargani, Aldo G. *Hobbes e la scienza.* Torino: Einaudi, 1971.
Spragens, Thomas A., Jr. *The Politics of Motion: The World of Thomas Hobbes.* Lexington: University Press of Kentucky, 1973.

Collections (in Chronological Order)

Hobbes Studies, ed. K. C. Brown. Oxford: Basil Blackwell, 1965.
Hobbes's Leviathan: Interpretation and Criticism, ed. Bernard H. Baumrin. Belmont, Calif.: Wadsworth, 1969.
Hobbes and Rousseau, ed. Maurice Cranston and Richard S. Peters. A collection of critical essays. Garden City, N.Y.: Doubleday, 1972.

Papers (in Alphabetical Order by Author)

Aaron, R. I. "A Possible Early Draft of Hobbes' *De Corpore,*" *Mind,* LIV (1945).
Barry, Brian. "Warrender and His Critics," *Philosophy,* XLIII (1968).
Bell, David R. "What Hobbes Does with Words," *Philosophical Quarterly,* XIX (1969).
Brown, K. C. "Hobbes's Grounds for Belief in a Deity," *Philosophy,* XXXVII (1962).
Brown, Stuart M., Jr. "Hobbes: The Taylor Thesis," *Philosophical Review,* LXVIII (1959).
Campbell, Blair. "Prescription and Description in Political Thought: The Case of Hobbes," *American Political Science Review,* LXV (1971).
Campbell, Enid. "Thomas Hobbes and the Common Law," *Tasmanian Law Review,* I (1958).
Engel, S. Morris. "Hobbes's Table of Absurdity," *Philosophical Review,* LXX (1961).
———. "Analogy and Equivocation in Hobbes," *Philosophy,* XXXVII (1962).
Gert, B. "Hobbes, Mechanism, and Egoism," *Philosophical Quarterly,* XV (1965).
———. "Hobbes and Psychological Egoism," *Journal of the History of Ideas,* XXVIII (1967).
Glover, Willis B. "God and Thomas Hobbes," *Church History,* XXIX (1960).
———. "Human Nature and the State in Hobbes," *Journal of the History of Philosophy,* V (1966).
Hungerland, Isabel C., and George R. Vick. "Hobbes's Theory of Signification," *Journal of the History of Philosophy,* XI (1973).
Krook, Dorthea. "Thomas Hobbes's Doctrine of Meaning and Truth," *Philosophy,* XXXI (1956).
Kuele, Martin. "Zwei Konzeptionen des Modernen Staats, Hobbes und Englische Juristen," *Studium Generale,* XXII (1969).
Lamprecht, S. P. "Hobbes and Hobbism," *American Political Science Review,* XXXIV (1940).
MacGillivray, Royce. "Thomas Hobbes's History of the English Civil War: A Study of Behemoth," *Journal of the History of Ideas,* XXXI (1970).
McNeilly, F. S. "Egoism in Hobbes," *Philosophical Quarterly,* XVI (1966).
Madden, E. H. "Thomas Hobbes in the Rationalistic Ideal," in *Theories of Scientific Method: The Renaissance through the Nineteenth Century.* Seattle: University of Washington Press, 1960.

Mansfield, Harvey C. "Hobbes and the Science of Indirect Government," *American Political Science Review*, LXV (1971).

Martin, R. M. "On the Semantics of Hobbes," *Philosophy and Phenomenological Research*, XIV (1953).

Mintz, Samuel. "Hobbes on the Law of Heresy: A New Manuscript," *Journal of the History of Ideas*, XXIX (1968).

———. "Hobbes's Knowledge of the Law of Heresy," *Journal of the History of Ideas*, XXXI (1970).

Moore, Stanley. "Hobbes on Obligation, Moral and Political. Part One: Moral Obligation," *Journal of the History of Philosophy*, IX (1971).

Oakeshott, Michael. Introduction to *Leviathan*. Oxford: Basil Blackwell, 1960.

———. "Moral Life in the Writings of Thomas Hobbes," in *Rationalism in Politics*. New York: Basic Books, 1962.

Olafson, Frederick A. "Thomas Hobbes and the Modern Theory of Natural Law," *Journal of the History of Philosophy*, IV (1966).

Parry, Geraint. "Performative Utterances and Obligation in Hobbes," *Philosophical Quarterly*, XVII (1967).

Passmore, J. A. "The Moral Philosophy of Hobbes," *Australasian Journal of Psychology and Philosophy*, XIX (1941).

Peters, R. S. and H. Tajfel. "Hobbes and Hull—Metaphysicians of Behavior," *British Journal of the Philosophy of Science*, VII (1957–58).

Pitkin, Hanna. "Hobbes's Concept of Representation—I," *American Political Science Review*, LVIII (June 1964).

———. "Hobbes's Concept of Representation—II," *American Political Science Review*, LVIII (December 1964).

Plamenatz, John. "Mr. Warrender's Hobbes," *Political Studies*, V (1957).

Polin, Raymond. "Le bien et le mal dans la philosophie de Hobbes," *Revue philosophique de la France et de l'etranger* CXXXVI (1946).

———. "La force et son emploi dans la politique de Hobbes," *Revue internationale de philosophie*, IV (1950).

Raphael, D. D. "Obligations and Rights in Hobbes," *Philosophy*, XXXVII (1962).

———. "Rationalism in Hobbes's Political Philosophy," in R. Loewe, *Studies in Rationalism, Judaism and Universalism*. New York: Humanities Press, 1966.

Scott, Frederick. "An Inconsistency in Hobbes's Nominalism," *Modern Scholastics*, XLIV (1967).

Skinner, Quentin. "Hobbes on Sovereignty: An Unknown Discussion" *Political Studies*, XIII (1965).

———. "The Ideological Context of Hobbes's Political Thought," *Historical Journal*, IX (1966).

———. "Thomas Hobbes and His Disciples in France and England," *Comparative Studies in Society and History*, VIII (1966).

Steadman, John M. "Leviathan and Renaissance Etymology," *Journal of the History of Ideas*, XXVIII (1967).

Taylor, A. E. "The Ethical Doctrine of Hobbes," *Philosophy*, XIII (1938).

Tornebahm, Hakou. "A Study in Hobbes' Theory of Denotation and Truth," *Theoria: Tidskrift för Filosofi och Psykologi*, XXVI (1960).

Warrender, Howard. "The Place of God in Hobbes's Philosophy, a Reply to Mr. Plamenatz," *Political Studies*, VIII (1960).

———. "Obligations and Rights in Hobbes," *Philosophy*, XXXVII (1962).

William, Robert. "Hobbes's Conception of Morality," *Rivista critica de storia della filosophia* (1962).

———. "Hobbes on the Law of Heresy," *Journal of the History of Ideas*, XXI (1970).
Williamson, Colwyn. "A Contradiction in Hobbes' Analysis of Sovereignty," *Canadian Journal of Economics and Political Science*, XXXII (1966).
———. "Watkins and the Taylor-Warrender Thesis," *Mind*, LXXVIII (1969).
———. "Hobbes on Law and Coercion," *Ethics*, LXXX (1970).

Index

INDEX